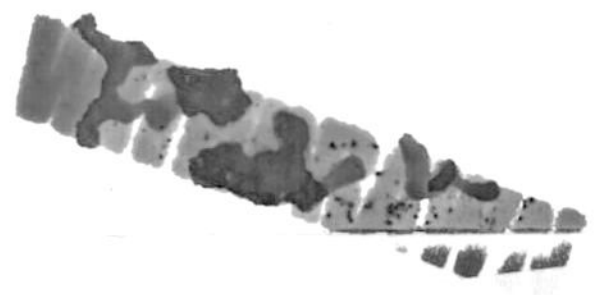

D0741921

SOUL MINING

SOUL MINING

A MUSICAL LIFE

DANIEL LANOIS

WITH KEISHA KALFIN

FABER AND FABER, INC.
AN AFFILIATE OF FARRAR, STRAUS AND GIROUX NEW YORK

Faber and Faber, Inc.
An affiliate of Farrar, Straus and Giroux
18 West 18th Street, New York 10011

Distributed in Canada by D&M Publishers, Inc.
Printed in the United States of America
First edition, 2010

Library of Congress Cataloging-in-Publication Data
Lanois, Daniel.
Soul mining : a musical life / Daniel Lanois.— 1st ed.
p. cm.
Includes index.
ISBN 978-0-86547-984-5 (hardcover : alk. paper)
1. Lanois, Daniel. 2. Singers—Canada—Biography. 3. Sound recording executives and producers—Canada—Biography. I. Title.

ML420.L239 A3 2010
781.64092—dc22
[B]

2010010278

Designed by Abby Kagan

www.fsgbooks.com

10 9 8 7 6 5 4 3 2 1

CONTENTS

SOUL MINING

1

FOUR KIDS AND FIVE HUNDRED MILES

The Ottawa River is the dividing line between Ontario and Quebec, or between English- and French-speaking Canada. When I was a child, as far as the eye could see, the river was often covered by miles and miles of floating logs making their way to the paper mill. That heavy sulfur smell in the air was taken for granted. The riverside road was flanked by log mountains, long-nosed cranes pouring their mysterious solution—one step closer to paper pulp. My parents lived on the Quebec side of the river, the French side, in a government housing community by the name of Projet Dusseau. We were French Canadian. I spoke only French until the age of ten, and I remember having a wonderful upbringing in that community. I never thought much about the fact that we were poor. Kids don't think that way.

The Quebec landscape was fascinating to me. Wooden bridges were covered up like birdhouses to keep the snow away. Wooden staircases with roofs were a common sight. *If the snow piles up too high, and the weather goes mild, you might not be able to get out till springtime. Chains wrapped around tires for better traction. Cars commonly equipped with tow ropes and battery booster cables. This maple-sugar country is very aware of the power of seasons.*

If you weren't ready for the winter, you could freeze and die. In those parts, preparation for survival comes naturally, even to a young boy. Preparation for survival is always in the wings, constantly kicking at your shin—even the shin of a young boy. When the thaw comes, you can hear the waking maples creaking, drinking in the snow water that creeps up the branches of dormant trees—that's how you get maple water. A spike in the tree interrupts the flow to the branches, and if your hillsides are clean, nature's nectar makes for a nice drink. The varying densities in the journey from maple water to maple syrup to maple sugar are dependent on how long one keeps the water boiling. Much like the winemaking valleys of France or the Bourbon-making valleys of Kentucky, the maple-sugar-making valleys of Quebec produce their limited quantities and fine vintages, with taste relative to the quality of the local soil, the intensity of the sun, and the tender love and care of a specific maple-sugar farm.

I remember the springtime ritual—the pouring of boiling maple water into the white snowbanks. As the water crystallizes against the snow, children run up with sticks and twirl the toffee into a homemade confection—nature's gift to the sweet tooth. Back in the day, my grandfather's sled—horse-drawn, hot bricks laid down beneath the feet of the passengers to keep everybody warm—was the family vehicle.

Sunday church runs, people wrapped in furs—the house of God was the house of cooperation. The priest's sermon could easily segue into village news: someone just had a baby, hand-me-down clothes needed, so-and-so's well just dried out, announcement of the church bazaar, help needed to raise a barn. Yes, the house of God was a crossing point for relevant village information. The barter system was in use then. My eggs for your wood, my plowing for your corn, and so on.

Every house was a food-making house, and my grandmother Aurore's house was no exception. She really knew how to work the maple sugar. Her *sucre à la crème* (maple sugar fudge), refined by generations of home recipes, was pretty much the best. At the savory end of the spectrum, my grandmother of course made *tourtière* (spicy meat pie). These old recipes were closely guarded. Boasting of a better *crème* or *tourtière* was not uncommon from one house to the next.

Kids walked to school in those days—I liked that about the project. We were on the edge of rural land and so my brother Bob and I wandered everywhere after school and did whatever we wanted. Many hours were spent by the railway tracks or at the river's edge doing boy things: skipping stones, laying pennies on the rail lines, watching them get squashed by the train. We were fascinated by the writing on the sides of the railcars, like Canadian Pacific Railway, Canadian National Rail; others were more specific to provinces and towns. Exotic names like Saskatoon, Thunder Bay, Wa Wa, and Mississauga sure stirred the imagination. Rolls of steel coming from the west, cattle cars, empty flatbeds, boxcars with open doors—we made up stories about their sources and destinations.

A ceramic tile factory by the name of Primco was our second backyard. Bob and I collected various discarded tiles and would make up games with them. A few of the Primco workers were sympathetic to our curiosity, slipping us a few irregular tiles to expand our little homemade building set. I loved the smell of that factory. They had kilns burning all the time, and the nonstop action appealed to me. It must have been a kick to see the faces of two brothers sticking their heads inside the Primco windows, looking for tile handouts. Even at that tender age, Bob and I loved the feeling of productivity.

It was a happy childhood, and I was oblivious to the fact that my parents were having marital problems, until I started hearing arguments in the night. Bob, my younger brother, Ron, and I slept in one room, and my parents slept in the other. The arrival of my sister, Jocelyne, meant that we had outgrown the two-bedroom place. Four kids and work not going all that well strained my parents' relationship, and then it all started. My dad was hitting not only the bottle, but also my mother. I later wrote a song about this called "Jolie Louise," the rise and fall of hopes and dreams as seen from the perspective of my dad.

Ma jolie, how do you do?
Mon nom est Jean-Guy Thibault-Leroux
I come from east of Gatineau
My name is Jean-Guy, ma jolie

J'ai une maison à Lafontaine
where we can live, if you marry me
Une belle maison à Lafontaine
where we will live, you and me
Oh Louise, ma jolie Louise

Tous les matins au soleil
I will work 'til work is done
Tous les matins au soleil
I did work 'til work was done
And one day, the foreman said
"Jean-Guy, we must let you go"
Et pis mon nom, y est pas bon
at the mill anymore . . .

Oh Louise, I'm losing my head,
I'm losing my head

My kids are small, four and three
et la bouteille, she's mon ami
I drink the rum 'til I can't see
It hides the shame Louise does not see
Carousel turns in my head,
and I can't hide, oh no, no, no, no
And the rage turned in my head
and Louise, I struck her down,
down on the ground
I'm losing my mind, I'm losing my mind

En Septembre '63
kids are gone, and so is Louise.
Ontario, they did go
near la ville de Toronto
Now my tears, they roll down,
tous les jours
And I remember the days,
and the promises that we made
Oh Louise, ma jolie Louise, ma jolie Louise

After my mother had had enough domestic mistreatment, she put the four kids on a train and took us from Quebec to Hamilton, Ontario—about a five-hundred-mile journey—and never looked back. Her brother had found work in Hamilton (near Toronto) as a bartender, and had managed to purchase a rooming house that we lived in the back of until my mom got on her feet. My dad was not happy about all of this, and so a few months later he came to fetch his boys. We were walking to school and he pulled up; we were happy to see him so we jumped in the car and that was it—five hundred miles back to Quebec. He put us in a cabin by a lake in rural Quebec, and that's where we lived for a good few months. My dad was doing carpentry work in town, and so during the week we lived by ourselves. He would come to visit on weekends—we had a blast. We were twelve, nine, and five.

My dad was a greaseball, as were his friends. They were the smart-dressing kind of greaseballs—no jeans. They were slick and dapper, and as this was the tail end of the fifties, there was a lot of excitement about cars. *A two-tone 1957 Chevy and all, lots of looking under the hood.* My dad was a good dancer. He was funny and looked sharp—very charming, and women like men who are charming. So much gets overlooked in the name of charm. It was a macho time and I liked it.

My dad and his friends were hunters. There was a lot of mythology about the *ways of the woods.* I remember my dad teaching me how to walk in the woods. He had learned from the Indians; it was all about being at one with the wilderness—one step and then a pause to listen. The results of the "listen" determine the next step, and then another "listen," and another step. Humans are only ever guests in the woods. In the way that a sailor never underestimates the power of the sea, the hunter never forgets the ways of the woods. Animals have much hearing power; they know a clumsy human intruder from far away. The listening pause between every step puts a human closer to the instinct of the animal.

Wintertime adds another dimension to the ways of the woods. The snowbanks hold secrets. One careless footstep might disturb the peace. Only experience can teach what terrain lies underneath the mysterious white snow. Snow time is better for tracking, but the advantage of seeing tracks in the soft surface could easily be crushed by a hunter's fall due to not understanding what lies underneath the beautiful white snow.

When the weather is hot, the flies can eat you alive. The sap running down from the pine trees could be your savior. Old Jocko Proux, one of the elders of the community, had survived the woods for an entire week by covering his whole body with pine sap as a barrier against the flies.

They say we walk in circles—we humans—in circles when we're lost. A marking on a white birch, connected with the marking on yet another white birch two hundred feet away, connected with a marking on yet another white birch another two hundred feet away, keeps a circling human going straight. The birch-to-birch technique is common knowledge as remedy for anyone lost in the woods.

Preparation is a big part of survival in these isolated northern Quebec communities, many of which have no electricity. The seasons are the governors and dictators of all human behavior. If you want ice for your icebox in the summer, then you must cut your ice from the lake in the winter. Ice cutting is a collective effort: a group of men, bucksaws in hand, cutting through two feet of ice. The ice is lifted out of the water with massive pliers and placed on skids to be dragged back to shore. The gaping hole has a slippery edge. One mistake and somebody might drown. This dangerous task is the cold-climate version of Mennonite community barn building—everybody chips in to fill one family's sawdust-filled cedar icehouse. Remarkably, the sawdust acts as an insulator and keeps the massive blocks of ice intact for the entire warm season. The family that does not fill their icehouse in the winter will not be able to keep their fish cold in the summer.

When my dad left us in the cabin, we pretty much did whatever we wanted. Bob and I shot rifles a lot, and Bob got really good—he could have been a sniper. I liked the smell of bullets exploding in my face. We three boys—we all loved shooting those rifles. We had a .303, a Winchester, and a .22. The .303 was a serious deer-hunting rifle, but even the .22 gave quite a kick because we shot .22 longs (these were the longer .22 shells for longer distance). There was a sandpit nearby where we shot arrows into the sky. We closed our eyes and waited for them to land, and sure enough they did, sometimes right next to us. It was a sort of "Quebec Roulette"—we could have gotten one in the head. What does all this mean? It just shows the madness of boys. Ron, the youngest, didn't do the arrow thing. He was busy cooking, five years old, standing on a chair at a woodstove. Everybody survived, and as crazy as it may seem, I believe those were good learning times.

My mother eventually came to steal us back, and so five hundred miles back to Hamilton. That was the end of the volley. I know my dad loved his kids, but I believe my mom did the right thing. It was all a bit mad, but I appreciate that my parents made decisions for themselves without the involvement of courtrooms. I have always been fascinated with the fact that people do not take responsibility for their actions. Some judge somewhere will decide what now needs to happen regarding a situation that you happily waltzed into? A completely personal matter will now be dealt with by some stranger? It all avalanches from there, lawsuits and accusations. My parents never spoke again. My dad didn't get pushed into any child-support scheme; it was a nice clear severance.

We resettled into Hamilton in my uncle's back apartment. It was a one-bedroom place. We three boys slept in the bedroom and my mom slept on a foldout couch with my sister. The boys' room had two bunk beds, and another bed in the corner. It was hard to adjust to the English language, but aside from that we had a good time. We walked to school, about a mile and a half. I loved walking, forever fascinated with the factories along the way. There was often a burning smell in the air, as Hamilton is a steelmaking town. We attended a French school, and our teachers were nuns. It was a big old place that had fallen into disarray and would soon be knocked down. Every kid brought a lunch bag from home, and when lunchtime rolled around, we ate at our desks. The school provided every kid with a little carton of milk. There was no refrigerator, and so the milk cartons were lined up on the windowsill to keep cool.

The school was closely associated with the church, and when the nuns concluded that I might be a candidate for the priesthood, I was introduced to some of the decision makers at the church. I remember a mild-mannered, curious man in a black robe, speaking tenderly as he pointed out paragraphs for me to read from the literature that he had brought. I was made to feel special, and I liked the idea of belonging to this club. They gave me an outfit, a robe with ornamental ribbons that I wore as they began to teach me the way of the altar. I became an altar boy, and the church was my hangout. It was like being backstage. There was wine, a few things to eat, and I got to ring the bells. I loved it. The priest would give me a wink, and I would whack the bells. Perhaps it was the camaraderie that appealed to me, like being in a band. This went on for a few years, until girls started looking more interesting than priests. That was the end of my priesthood.

Back in Quebec, music had been all around me. My dad was a *violoneux*, which means a violin player or fiddler, as was his dad, my grandfather. Grandfather Lanois was good on the violin, and though he was not a professional, he played at neighborhood events, weddings, and other ceremonies. On my mom's side there were singers. My uncles and aunts sang old Quebec folk songs, and it all added up to a self-entertaining environment. Our gatherings were typical of the Quebec culture of the time. *Big families, late-night card playing, lots of laughing, shouting, banging on tables, kids piled up in the bed while the adults went crazy in the other room. No babysitters—people didn't use babysitters.*

The music of Quebec has always stayed with me, especially the melodies, and although I didn't play an instrument yet, I was already thinking about music. I wanted a clarinet, which somewhere along the way I had gotten it into my head that I should play. Probably something I saw on television.

My mother allowed me one dollar a week as personal spending money, and I spent it on Saturdays when I would walk downtown by myself and see a movie. This was the time of biblical movies, so I got to see films like *David and Goliath* and *Samson*. I loved them. I thought they were sexy—robes, skimpy outfits, and pretty girls. On one Saturday, walking to the cinema, I was distracted by a plastic pennywhistle in the front window of a music store. It was white plastic with red finger holes. It didn't look quite like a clarinet, but it was close. The price tag on it said one dollar. On that Saturday, I didn't make it to the movies—but I did walk through the door that led me to a new life.

My little plastic pennywhistle and me. My new companion that I played nonstop for the next two years. In order to remember melodies, I invented a notation system. It looked something like this:

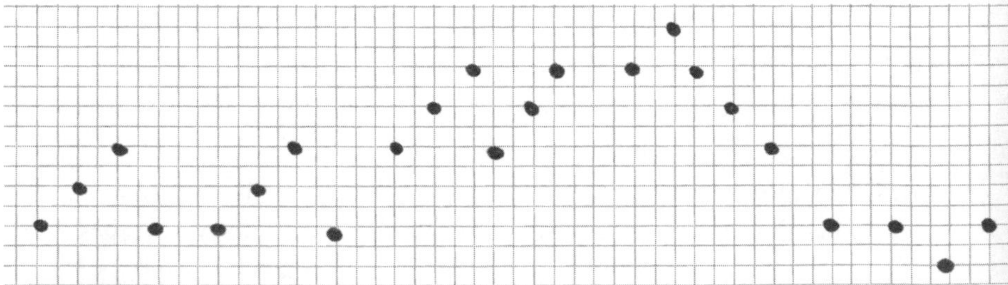

The first dot on the left related to a specific fingering on my pennywhistle, and then, much like the reading of a sentence, I would read it left to right; my melody was now carved in stone. That seemed to work pretty well as a way of remembering. This little self-made system was my way of remembering what was important to me.

This next diagram is a two-page memo that I pulled out of a workbook of mine, circa 1984. The diagram includes song-structure reminders plus various ideas relating to further development of the song.

This diagram precedes the recording of the final version of U2's song "Pride (in the Name of Love)." Note-keeping is a big part of what I do. There is nothing like being fully informed: knowledge equals ease of operation.

This sort of diagram dominates my workbooks. Sometimes they are enough to make me crazy, but I've never known a way around them. Keeping track of arrangements and ideas on paper has always been part of my work process. *Remembering* is just another word for choosing. The world turns the same way for everybody but different people choose to see different things. I decided to remember the little pieces that matter to me. This is the same way that I see God, as little pieces flying by, tiny molecular pieces of information constantly flying by. Some people see them, some people don't. *A godly moment may be sparkling in only a tiny way—too small to make a difference in its singular form—but stacked up with others the sparkle begins to build shapes. The shapes are the instigators of sound, soul, and dreams. Dreams allow you to then see more possibilities, and in my case, my dreams become realities. Not quickly, maybe only one piece at a time over, say, three years, before it all falls together.*

I have discovered that many of my collaborators were also obsessed with documentation, even as children. The Edge, of U2,

Average speed 18-18

John	1	room 1	eight figure	
"	"	"	2	shuted eighths
John	2	"	1	mixed up
"	"	"	2	and left out
John	4	"	1	not good
"	"	"	2	not good
John	5	"	1	muted ?
"	"	"	2	bad

Pride

Recut track at Windmill. Perhaps deep snare would apply best. Also deep bass. Experiment with placement of drums.

Bass is sounding good at back of of studio therefore drums placed in reception may be the best idea. Why not isolate gtr as well. Perhaps musicians standing in reception with access to ? with access to their amplifiers via the back door and the studio door.

there is when Bono make vocal entire mistake

proposed soft verse lengthened

proposed extended chorus

intro, verse, chorus, verse, chorus, bridge, bridge, intro, verse, chorus, bridge, bridge, chorus, chorus

15, 27, 45, 102, 122, 140, 156, 215, 220, 304, 330, 344, 400, 410, 448

8, 8, 8, 8, 8, 8, 8, 8, 16, 8, 8, 8, 8, 8, 8

Phil Spector tamb ½ time sound fills in choruses

Boomerang

Decide on either band room or studio.
Drum dub treatments will work well, set time aside for this. Also time for Larry percussion
A.M.S. loops on ac gtr band version
Vocal long lines start on 4 of bar before chord change
Hi-hat dubs triplets and steam

Pride demo drum format

intro — roll — roll — roll — roll — roll

C B V C B C

8ths, 16ths, 8ths T, 16ths 16ths, 8ths, 8ths T, 16ths 16ths, 8ths is such a man. His notes regarding composition and arrangements are forensic. Eno is a master of the pen. His books are incredible, complete with intricate diagrams to support his theories. I suppose this is the sort of process one learns in university, but why wait for university when you can figure it out as a teenager?

A man knocked on my mother's door and asked if she had any kids that liked music. She said that she had one who liked to play the pennywhistle. Having passed the aptitude test, the man explained to my mother that his school taught only accordion and slide guitar. Accordion didn't appeal to me, and so I became a slide guitar player. Now, once a week, I was walking to my music lesson carrying an acoustic guitar with very high action—the strings were about an inch off the neck—and I played it with a steel bar. I loved it.

My teacher was a curious man who experimented with hypnotism. At the beginning of every lesson, he would hypnotize me by placing a little object on the music stand as a focal point. He made me look at it until everything got blurry, as he repeated "you're getting sleepy." Once I was hypnotized, the lesson would start, and sure enough, it worked. I got really good on the slide, and my interest in music broadened by the week. I now lived in the most incredible world, up at 4:00 a.m. to deliver the morning paper, and then rushing home to open the cases of my pennywhistle and slide guitar. I loved the smell of them, and I played these instruments until my fingers bled and my mind got sharp.

My brother Bob and I are of similar mind. It's the kind of mind that dismantles the engine of the family car and then reassembles it before my mother gets home. *The mind that looks at the electrical transformer up on a pole and figures out high-voltage current reduction to 220 and then down to 110. The kind of mind that memorizes the complicated morning paper route. That memorizes each and every name of each customer. The mind that wants to know what goes on behind the doors of factory buildings, wants to know the sidelines of the steel business in Hamilton and how they make wire all stacked up in a yard on large industrial spools. The mind that wants to know the next newspaper customer. The customer range was wide. My factory and industrial clients were reliable, but my drunk customers living in the York Street Hotel were not. Much of my time was spent banging on doors in smelly hallways, trying to collect from transient customers. Rooms by the week, rusted-out Cadillacs, barflies drowning sorrows—this sketchy part of town sure was an education for an eleven-year-old.*

Through my little grapevine, I had heard about the job opportunity. A kid in school who was a little older than me was moving away, and he made his newspaper route available to me. A hundred and twenty copies of *The Globe and Mail* every morning made for a big route, but I took it on anyhow. Every morning I woke up at 4:00 or 5:00, put on my warm clothes, and put my wire-cutting key in my pocket. I headed for the newspaper drop-off, my route in my head. I always worried that I might not remember the address of every customer, and the seasons dictated whether I could use my bicycle or not. If I couldn't use the bike, I carried the papers in a sack—120 papers cutting into my shoulder. My morning route afforded me some isolated time away from adults, time for a child's imagination to grow. There's something powerful that happens when you rise before the rest of the world. The feeling of freedom or rebirth that I imagine the birds feel every morning also belongs to a newspaper delivery boy. *The two voices or characters in my head would inevitably start talking. They would argue and discuss, the one trying to outwit the other, or win the argument, both characters played by myself. Is this a mental illness? Or a necessary preparation for the psychological journey one must embark on to be good in the recording studio? I still play the two characters today. Sometimes I get strange looks from people.*

I was trying to find a place in the world, as were my brothers. My sister was just a baby then, raised by my grandmother while my mother worked. My grandmother was beautiful, with an oversized thumb, three times bigger than a normal one—I never knew why. She sang while doing the dishes. Everything pretty much happened in one room—one big kitchen with a porch to sit out on. The backyard was pretty, a yard that we shared with my grandmother because her apartment was right next door. My grandmother Aurore kept a bird; she loved that bird. I love birds too—my affection for them must come from Aurore. As the world trips over itself, chasing the latest gadget, the birds do what they've always done.

My brother Bob was always the scientist of us two. We were pretty much inseparable once we got our recording studio going. Bob and I would stay up late nights challenging every situation with bright ideas. I love all ideas, even absurd ones. After all, pushing the envelope is such a large part of innovation. Bob and I always had a tape recorder around the house. Our first one was an old flea-market machine, everything on board—microphone, speakers—really easy to use. It had a warbly, muted sound. My friends would come over, and we'd have a laugh recording our voices and listening back.

My next setup was in the basement. The machine was a Roberts, again with onboard speakers. Reel to reel, quarter-inch quarter-track, which meant you could flip the reel over and record more music using the same spool. My next rig was great, a Sony TC-630. Again fully contained, mics, speakers, the lot, except it had a "sound on sound" feature. I had now found my secret weapon. The Sony allowed me to record on channel 1, and then on listening back I could transfer that sound onto channel 2, along with some more singing or playing in the room. A miracle! I could now stack up tracks by bouncing from channel to channel. A technological deficiency became my friend. The more transferring I did, the more muted the early recordings became. This meant that the earlier parts became more faraway sounding, giving the last part added a more upfront, brighter, closer-sounding position. Voila! Auto-mixing and automatic "depth of field." I began to plan my recordings in anticipation of this deficiency. I would stack up my performances but wait to record my up-front information as my last layer. This was also an excellent training for commitment to a blend. Mixing along the way became part of my technique then and is still with me today.

The "sound on sound" technique also persisted, even into the next chapter of my career. At this point, Bob and I had purchased two Revox quarter-inch recorders, excellent Swiss machines. We would record onto the first Revox, and if we liked the result, we would record more playing and singing on top as we transferred onto the second Revox. The quality was amazing—nice, big, punchy, full sound. At any stage of the transfer system, you could decide that that was enough, and that was it. The final Revox recording became the master tape. This was a big thrill, and the buzz was out—the Lanois brothers had built a sound. People came from all over the place to record in my mom's basement. We took it a step further, and offered a package vinyl deal. Two days in the studio, artwork, and a thousand pieces of vinyl delivered to your door. Our little business started to boom.

The next setup was a four-track. Our homemade console was built by two local technicians and my brother Bob; it was originally created with a stereo output, but Bob later modified it to accommodate the four-track Teac. The Teac, of course, could only hold so much information, and so Bob and I invented the six-track system. Legato information, like strings or background vocals, would be mixed down to the Revox, freeing up tracks for more recording on the Teac. The strings and the background vocals would just sit on the Revox until the mix. Come mixing time, a single large button triggered the Teac and Revox to start at the same time, with the help of china marks on the tapes. If the markings were accurate, it would all be in sync, and the six tracks were then combined onto the other Revox. Magic! Production was now complete with strings and background vocals.

The four-track studio is where I recorded Rick James. Rick lived in Buffalo, New York, which is located on the Canada/United States border not far from the burbs of Hamilton, where our studio was located. A friend of mine, Eddie Roth, was playing organ with Rick and recommended my studio as a cool place to make demos.

The master musical mind of Rick James is still with me today. He was a monster arranger, full productions pouring out of the speakers within twenty minutes. I felt like I was in the presence of Bach or Beethoven. His understanding of the tapestry of funk in my experience remains unparalleled. Rick breezed in and out of my life but remains one of my great teachers. I didn't even mind that Rick never paid me for the session.

The nonstop flow of people in and out of my mother's house was incredible; the place became a hangout. My mother even cooked for clients. The kitchen table that had seen everything was about to see even more. I can't imagine what the neighbors were thinking—what was Rick James doing in their neighborhood? The house had only one bathroom, and as I think about it now, the invasion of privacy was something that my mom could easily have been angry about, but she reversed the energy and embraced the entire situation. Some of the recording sessions, like the Jamaican reggae sessions, accommodated up to thirty people. Picnic blankets on the front lawn, immediate and extended families all welcome. When nighttime came, they'd end up watching TV in my mother's front room. It was not a regular house.

The basement studio hosted the recordings of hundreds of albums, including a lot of gospel quartets. The quartets were a big part of my education. The four parts keep the brain sharp, the melody is being chased constantly by the three harmonies. Occasionally, the melody may even become subservient to the harmony. What an amazing world of invention! I believe my ability to come up with harmonies has a lot to do with these early lessons.

I should mention something here about Raffi. Raffi was a folksinger from Toronto who decided to make a record for kids. His wife was a teacher, so he had a connection to the school system. In 1976, Raffi, Ken Whiteley, and I recorded an album called *Singable Songs for the Very Young.* If I remember right, we gave Raffi a package deal, all-inclusive—studio time and all the help I could give him, beginning to end, for $1,500. That's the way it was done then, a nice clean deal everybody was happy with. The record went on to sell millions. We were rootin' for Raffi. We made three other albums together. They all shot through the roof. Raffi's kindness guided him to humanitarian work that he involves himself with to this day. He remains the king of kid's music.

Our drum kit was surrounded by egg crates that I had purchased from the egg man; the crates were meant to deaden the spitting high frequencies. The microphone technique seems curious to me now. I think we could safely say that faith was the major ingredient in my drum sound of the time (see the cover of this book for an illustration). The studio also had an upright Japanese piano that I sweated over many long nights, trying to tune the thing for the morning session. I couldn't afford a piano tuner, so I learned how to do it myself.

Old Man Baker, who lived two streets over, was a harpsichord builder who didn't like wood; he liked metal. His heart had been broken too many times by wood, with its never-ending swelling and contracting relative to the level of humidity in the air. He was now building harpsichords out of metal. Old Man Baker broke the rule of the suburbs. Rather than the obligatory manicured front lawn, he opted for a jungle of spices, veggies, and fruits, including grapes. Constantly drunk on homemade wine, he ranted on about his metal-versus-wood theories. He was an outrageous character, and his house, like my mother's, was often a home for wayward teenagers. Everybody thought he was a kook, but in retrospect he was the only guy in the neighborhood who made any sense.

Old Man Baker taught me the theory of equal temperament, which was designed to accommodate any key on the piano. It works like this: first you tune middle C to your tuning fork, and then you tune the next C an octave above it, also to the tuning fork, which means those two notes are now perfectly in tune, and not to be changed. The E note above middle C will now be tuned by ear, so that it sounds nice when played with middle C. The relationship between middle C and the E is described as a major third. Now that the E sounds nice against the C, we must make the G-sharp above the E also sound nice. In other words, the relationship between the E and the G-sharp needs to sound as pleasing as the relationship between the C and the E. Once we have that, the C above the G-sharp, which we already tuned to the tuning fork and which cannot be changed, must sound nice against the G-sharp. If the C does not sound nice against the G-sharp, then we must backtrack and alter the E a little bit, and then alter the G-sharp a little bit, until the relationship sounds equally good between all three intervals. This is called dividing up the octave.

The terrible part about all this is that each of these intervals will sound just a little sour to the ear. Long ago Western music decided to embrace a grand compromise in the name of flexibility. The result was that every major chord will be a little out of tune in itself: i.e., the third of any major triad will always be a little bit sharp. This is enough to make me crazy, as I am a pedal steel guitar player, and my ear constantly searches for perfect pitch. I don't like compromise, but the flaw in equal temperament suggests that compromise must be lived with.

We eventually moved into a new studio on Grant Avenue. By that time Bob and I had moved up to a sixteen-track American recorder made by MCI. The console was also MCI. Bob built the new studio while I kept going in the basement. The renovations exceeded our budget, and we were pushed to accept a second mortgage at a rate of 17 percent, an insane amount that we paid for years.

The habit from my newspaper route of getting up very early was still with me, except now I was up at four in the morning to go to the studio and work on my sounds. I had early sampling gear that I was excited about. In fact, the term *sample* had not been invented yet—I called them traps. I would catch little fragments from vinyl records and then manipulate my sources to the point of nonrecognition. These experiments were made prior to my meeting Eno.

Brian Eno became aware of my work while he lived in New York City. I had recorded some inventive demos with a group from Toronto called the Time Twins. My friend Billy Bryans had in fact produced these demos, and they were full of sonic delights and the songs themselves were very unusual. The Twins took their wares to New York and somehow bumped into Eno. They played him the tapes, and he was curious about where they were made. The Twins told Eno that a kid from Canada named Danny

Lanois made them in his studio. Coincidentally, Eno was planning a trip to Toronto, and he chance-booked a session with me. I had never heard of him, and so I advised Bob to insist that Eno bring cash. He turned out to be a reliable sort and initiated a major turning point in my life.

Eno came into my world as an incredible force of work ethic and dedication. Time stood still as I became a conduit for the most progressive thinking I had ever been exposed to. Before Eno, I had been in a sort of limbo, building my skills but not with any specific direction. Eno arrived with a suitcase full of bells, acquired on Canal Street in New York. The first thing he said to me was that he wanted to record the bells as he walked around the studio for forty-five minutes, the idea being that the bells would ring throughout the entire record. I set up six microphones and Eno proceeded to walk around as I recorded. There were a few creaks in the floor that I had never noticed before, because people don't usually walk around studios. The bells were meant to be a companion to the 7½ IPS tapes that Eno had brought with him from New York. As I transferred them to my sixteen-track recorder, they revealed the most beautiful, delicate, melodic, and romantic piano playing, which sounded like a sort of contemporary version of the great French composer Eric Satie. The artist was Harold Budd.

Punk had just exploded and anger seemed to be a common ingredient in the music I had been recording in the few years preceding the Eno visit. The Eno/Budd work had no anger in it. It had stillness, acceptance, and premonition. It had patience, subtlety, and refinement. The anger was left outside in the busy hustling world. My heart rate slowed down and time stood still. The vibe got thicker by the day. I began to live for nothing else—I cared only about the work. I felt like a forensic expert or a scientist or a doctor, on the verge of solving some great, menacing riddle.

Eno's early years had been very different from mine. He had gone to art school, and so had a broad knowledge of art and contemporary urban philosophies and trends. He had already recorded some very significant records—some of Talking Heads' best work, *Remain in Light*, for example; *My Life in the Bush of Ghosts* with David Byrne; David Bowie classics like *Low*, *Lodger*, and *Heroes*, and Brian's own records, of course, like *Before and After Science*, *Another Green World*, and *Music for Airports*, all regarded as groundbreaking. I was highly skilled but isolated and not aware of the revolution that Eno had been a part of.

Years of preparation and skill-building had now found a home. I loved working with Eno. He came in like a breath of fresh air, like some sort of redemption after many years of laboring through bill-paying projects. Brian's work did not accommodate the expectations of pop music; it was something timeless. Finally I felt that my work had relevance. Eno was about to be my teacher—not of music, not of the recording process, but my teacher of dedication and belief. Choose your passion and enter the arena! One note of Harold Budd's piano crushed the back of years of struggle and disappointment. I felt I was on my way.

Eno liked the fact that I was musical. Yes, I was a good technician—but more important, I was a musician. Perhaps this is the right time to talk about faith. Being faithful to skill-building without knowledge of practical future application has always been part of me. Running on excitement, I will pursue a skill or an idea, trusting that one day it will find a home.

My tools have always been dear to me, and I continue to embrace tools—technology and musical instruments—as they come my way. Back in the late sixties I purchased my first steel guitar from the great Canadian steel guitarist Bob Lucier. Bob was playing at the Edison, a country music club near the Brown Derby, where I was playing in a show band to make some cash. This was all happening on Yonge Street in Toronto, pretty much at the sunset of the great Toronto nightclub era. Levon Helm explains it beautifully in his book *This Wheel's on Fire.*

Lucier was a god to me. His calmness and harmonious way of playing appealed to me. He was also a "Frenchy," and so I was instantly comforted by his French Canadian accent. He spoke slowly like me, and had a machinist's way of explaining the workings of the steel guitar. Bob agreed to teach me the ins and outs of the steel, and offered to supply me with my first Sho-Bud. He was kind and wise, and I felt a fatherly embrace in his guidance. When you don't grow up with a father around, you notice these fatherly moments, even from strangers. Bob was a force and I looked forward to my weekly lesson with him.

The emptiness that I had reached with church during my school years had now been filled with joy by Bob Lucier. I played my little Sho-Bud bird's-eye maple guitar and all kinds of pictures came into my mind about the future. I saw myself playing with Dolly Parton, with my name written across the front of my guitar, just as I'd seen on TV. Maybe I could be on the Porter Wagoner show. Maybe I could be on TV with Willie Nelson or with the "Sweetheart of America," Emmylou Harris.

My early studies in finger picking sure helped me out. All of a sudden, years of classical guitar training made sense. I was able to skate around the steel like a magician. My right hand was advanced and took quickly to the steel. I could play in an original way because I did not come up in the conventional steel guitar manner.

My tone was full and deep—I wasn't fast, but I had tone. The years of radio listening in my mother's basement had taught me that it took very little to make a listener feel something. Fewer notes were often better; like Albert King or John Lee Hooker or Booker T. Heartfelt strokes would outlast speed. I had reached a crossroads in my musical life, another pivotal moment of clarity. The steel would be my "Church in a Suitcase" and a friend for the rest of my life.

The Eno sessions dominated my time, and I was glad that Bob was taking care of business. Eno, my brother, and I developed a friendship—we became the dedicated men of ambient music. Eno had been working on his ambient music theory for some time. Years before, he had been hit by a taxicab in London. While lying in the hospital bed he noticed that the classical music playing over the speaker in his room was audible only at the crescendos of the arrangements. In the quieter passages, there was seemingly silence, but as the orchestra ramped up its energy, a moment would rear its head—the loud passages were the only audible bits. The randomness of the risings appealed to Eno. He liked the fact that the music was not constant, like a gentle wind blowing a sweet scent your way, which then disappears and reappears. This was the beginning of Eno's Ambient Music Theory.

By 1980, Eno and I were working together regularly. He came up from New York as often as he could and we continued with the ambient recordings. Eno had been invited to supply music for a documentary about the Apollo space missions, and as this was intriguing to him, he accepted. The ambient music makers were now about to create music for outer space.

There was a country-music tone to the space project because the astronauts were from Texas. The banter between the astronauts and ground control all had a bit of a twang to it. My steel guitar had found a new home. Eno encouraged me to overdub on a dreamy celestial track called "Deep Blue Day" to complement a piano track played by his brother, Roger, who also had been invited to Canada to join in on the project. "Deep Blue Day" became an ambient classic thirteen years later after it was used in the toilet bowl scene in the film *Trainspotting.* My steel guitar may have been memorialized by a toilet bowl, but "Deep Blue Day" is still one of my favorite instrumentals. The album ultimately was named *Apollo*, and is a memorable journey through space. *Apollo* also includes "An Ending Ascent," one of my favorite creations by Eno. A good many ambient records were made during this chapter of innovation, and as always, dedicated work segues into a next chapter. We were now about to bring ambience to Dublin.

Eno received an invitation in 1983 to produce a record for a new band in Ireland called U2. He agreed to a meeting and asked if I could come along as we were on a creative roll: the "Ambient Junkies" were now in Dublin. We found ourselves crammed in a car with all the U2 guys and Eno and I in the backseat, cassettes being played at full volume, Bono shouting melodies and making up choruses. It was all a bit mad, but very exciting. Bono's enthusiasm was contagious, and even though we didn't hear finished songs, there seemed to be enough to go on. Eno had originally planned on introducing me to U2, and then thought he would walk away and leave me with the project. I suppose that all changed in the heat of the moment and he finally said yes. All crunched up in the back of the car, I nodded my head and somehow I was now on board with Eno and U2.

2

SLING BLADE

Sometimes things in your life just line up in a way you don't expect, but that you somehow initiate based on a gut feeling. Back in Canada, before meeting U2, I had been experimenting with making recordings in Hamilton's old disused library. The library had relocated and the massive architecturally significant edifice had become my playground for sonic experimentation. It was the setting for the making of a rock 'n' roll record with a local Hamilton band called Common Language. I loved the library for its endless possibilities for sound. There were all kinds of fascinating hallways, back rooms, and mezzanines. The suffocation I had felt in a dead, padded studio was no longer with me. I became addicted to having a broad palette of possibilities.

Coincidentally, U2 were also interested in recording outside the formal studio. Perhaps this was another sign that we were destined to collaborate. When they mentioned Slane Castle (on Ireland's River Boyne) as a location, I felt that my instincts regarding alternative location recording had allowed me to step into the future. (Sometimes there is no rhyme or reason to a maneuver, but you feel something, and so you chase up an idea, even if it doesn't seem practical.)

There have been other coincidences regarding the design of my shop. I had no idea what was going to happen when I rented an old Mexican cinema house on the Pacific Coast Highway, in a town called Oxnard in California. I've always loved cinema houses, and so when I saw the marquee of the Teatro with a "For Rent" sign on it, I rolled the dice and moved in with my studio. Little did I know that the Teatro would play a substantial role in the building of Bob Dylan's *Time Out of Mind*. Little did I know that the Teatro was about to be a composer's dream location for Billy Bob Thornton's *Sling Blade* soundtrack.

When an invitation came to compose the music for *Sling Blade*, I felt that I had built the perfect shop for the project. To make a movie soundtrack in a movie theater—genius! I was sent a copy of *Sling Blade* to watch, a curious view of America through the eyes of a mentally handicapped man, just released from the insane asylum, who returns to society after having been locked up for thirty years. I never would have thought my music could fit such a story. I watched *Sling Blade* with my Canadian friend Brian Patti. He loved it and advised me to take the project on. Billy Bob called and asked if I liked the film—I told him I did. Billy talked about the commitment he and all those involved had poured into the film so far and asked if he could expect the same commitment from me. I told him "yes, of course"; he could expect at least that. I was now Billy's composer.

The spirit of the Teatro was such that it had performance breathing from the walls. Having no natural light proved to be an asset; it allowed for a consistency in mood. My old friend and engineer Mark Howard helped me chip away at the aesthetics. Parachutes, purchased at the army surplus store down the street and hung from the ceiling, helped in deadening high-frequency spitting and also looked pretty. The theater had a stage with long maroon velvet curtains and a huge screen, and also an orchestra pit.

Howard and I had set up weather balloons as surfaces for 16 mm film projections. We sat the balloons on drainpipes six feet high and eighteen inches across standing up. The balloons on the pipes were like large crystal balls. The spheres each had two images, front and back (if a sphere can have a front and back). Our projections onto them were alive, two projections for the price of one. It's hard to describe the mysterious, awesome result, kind of like floating images from an unknown source. It was a playground of musical instruments, motorcycles, and art. How good does it get!

Howard had picked up a cheap remote switcher that would command various relays around the place, turning equipment on and off remotely. During playback, he would be at the helm and part of his duty was to provide a light show as he saw fit. We had 16 mm loops of all kinds—old boxing movies mixed with curious newsreels from the forties.

All around the place, we had couches and diner booths elevated to different heights on risers, like a cool old Cuban nightclub. Our fleet of motorcycles flanked the entranceway, along with my 1959 Brunswick pool table, waiting to lure visitors into a humbling ass-kicking by Danny La Noise. The bathroom was a cave with mood lighting and my Nikon 35 mm military-grade camera set up with a foot-switch remote and an invitation to create a self-portrait. We were not about to be accused of peeping through a hole in the wall—every bathroomgoer was now in charge of their own peeping. Lots of cool pictures came out of that.

The rear of the Teatro housed my Dutch PA back system. Four 18-inch subwoofers and two tops, all self-powered. Not many studios can boast a full-scale PA sound. The Teatro had it. The front stacks were made of two Claire Brothers subs and Westlake tops, the same models I used on U2's *The Joshua Tree*. Rigged and flown above the middle area were two EV Sentry 500s, great speakers that have since been discontinued. So there it was—a kickass surround-sound system, better than you would likely hear anywhere in a room of that size. At any point, the power of this sound system could turn the Teatro into a pounding nightclub—sometimes pumping up the volume is the best way to inspire performance.

We were interested in accommodating visitors at this shop. It would not only be a place of privacy for recording, it would be a place of performing for a crowd. Bleachers, couches, cinema stock seating, and old massive dining booths from the Mexican restaurant across the street made it possible to seat, say, two hundred people. The speaker system that I just described would reach all listeners but still feel intimate. This was my way of protesting the ineffective front-speaker-stack system that pretty much all live performance places embraced. The front speaker stack is good for about twenty rows. If you're not in the lucky front twenty rows, it gets hard to hear the words of the song. It's all pretty simple: bass frequencies travel far, high frequencies don't. If you want your audience to hear what you're singing about, then you better get a speaker near them, speakers right by them—say five or ten feet, max. Don't make them strain to hear what you're talking about. In the Teatro, my surround-sound dream had come true.

For Billy Bob and *Sling Blade*, I assembled an orchestra of Canadian musicians, and there was definitely a clubhouse vibe. I put the musicians in the motel next door, kind of a seedy-hooker place, but they seemed to be happy enough with it. The good thing about the Canadians was that they were happy to be dedicated solely to this project. I had worked out a package deal with them, and they were ready to live and breathe only for *Sling Blade*. I have never liked the idea of employing studio musicians by the hour. It works best for me when I assemble a group of folks dedicated solely to the project.

Some of the compositions for *Sling Blade* were made without the orchestra. I would rise up in the night from the orchestra pit and plug into my ever-evolving guitar rig. At the time I was very excited about a recording box called the Boomerang. This would allow me to record a chord sequence and then play on top of it without anyone else in the room. This brought back memories of some of my very early recording rigs when I was a kid. The sound-on-sound technique that I used back then was still with me twenty years later at the Teatro.

Billy would roll down with a jar of white lightning, some kind of hard-hitting stuff that a friend of his had brought back from Arkansas. Billy was having migraines then, and there were times when I didn't know if he was in the Teatro or not. He would pass out upstairs in the projector booth and then wake up half a day later and be standing there like a ghost. I never knew where he lived then, but I can remember having long conversations with him. He would call from a phone booth because he didn't like to be in his house much. I had this strange view of him, like he was some sort of a nowhere man.

Some people have said that Billy and I look similar. I've seen the resemblance myself in photographs, but I think the real resemblance lies in obsession. We are similar in our fundamental values of kindness and lust for quality. Some late nights at Billy Bob's (I'm talking up-all-night late nights) have slowly revealed what's underneath his character, and, for that matter, mine. Billy said to me that some built-in anger in our beings had yet to be exorcised, and as much as we are driven by the wonderful vehicles of music and film, we are still only trying to burn out the anger. I'm still trying to figure out what anger Billy's talking about, but I have to say I can't disagree with him. There are times when something takes over, and I become this other person. I usually just ask this other person if he can play guitar and make records, and he always says yes. This can be an interesting experience because I get to sit on the sidelines and watch the angry guy work. It's a curious experiment, relative to the fuel poured in—a few espressos and you get theories, pour in a few whiskeys and you'll get the rebel mind.

The late night continued—Billy weaved his hands in front of his face. There it was, that little shining moment of liftoff. Billy went on talking about the lens. The single camera perspective appealed to him as a filmmaker. Why couldn't the camera move around the room relative to the action? The community that relies on three or four cameras for cross-editing purposes might never get the magic of the single moving camera. "Whoever made up the rule *Never look in the lens*?" Billy says. "I look in the lens all the time, it's another dimension, like looking into somebody's soul."

The quiet moments of nonaction in a film are storytelling moments for Billy. Hearing somebody breathe, a split second of doubt, looking across the room for reassurance, finding it in someone, and throwing the ball back. I've thrown the ball back at Billy many times, and he has done it for me. Two people in a room can make for the best volley. The relationship that Billy and I had on *Sling Blade* avoided compromise. The one-on-one director-composer relationship is the best. I had it with Billy on the *Sling Blade* soundtrack, Wim Wenders had it with Ry Cooder on *Paris, Texas*, and Fellini had it with Nino Rota on *Juliet of the Spirits*. It's a wonderful feeling to know that you're at one with your mate. Too often I've felt the opposite: decisions made in boardrooms, democracy at its worst. Billy and I keep threatening to realign our singularities. I hope to make a soundtrack for him one day made up of pure steel guitar. Billy and I are both birdmen, or perhaps we ourselves are birds, still in cages. I always say goodbye to Alice when I'm leaving Billy's house, his mynah bird in a cage, a mynah bird as a butler.

Billy loved the Teatro. He loved the roughness of it, that it was continuously evolving and blowing through the confinements of design. Studio designs assume that you know what you want ahead of time. But what about what you don't know? That's the part that interests me—the unknown. The Teatro was all about the unknown. Located inconveniently far away from L.A. in Oxnard, the possibility of a chance meeting was nonexistent. You had to be self-contained, technologically and emotionally.

The opening piece of music in *Sling Blade* invokes a dark, menacing, haunting mood, built with my Boomerang and Les Paul rig. Howard would crawl into the Teatro in the morning and proceed to his station to further manipulate my discoveries. No multitrack was used for this composition; it was essentially a live performance. Every stage of the Boomerang lasted roughly forty-five seconds, every new stage accommodated the preceding one. Each stage would be a roll of the dice because if you made a mistake, you'd have to start all over again.

Howard would manipulate as I contemplated the introduction of the next stage. This opening piece of music is called "Asylum." I believe it is one of the most reaching pieces of music I've ever created, very much in the Eno tradition, built with just a few tools, but with much concentration. "Asylum" runs through the entire beginning of Billy's movie. It sets a tone, keeps you on the edge of your seat, like a snowbank crystallizing and cracking in the sun.

Any suggestion that Billy Bob had could be instantly put into play, as we had all the players and equipment right there. There were many moments of spontaneity. Billy Bob would listen to my melodies and choose his favorites, suggesting variations for other scenes. This unorthodox approach seemed appropriate to Billy Bob's renegade way of thinking. *Sling Blade* had been made with love and passion, and the love and passion continued at the Teatro.

My sound equipment was sophisticated, but my film equipment was crude. Billy would bring by a VHS with scenes on it and our little orchestra would play the music while watching the tape. I didn't bother using any time code or anything; we would simply use a visual cue point to start up the band. If it all worked out, we would make Billy a VHS dub with my music on it for him to take home. Billy would then pass that VHS on to his editor and the editor would simply replicate the starting point of the music for the picture.

Magic was in the air and momentum was working in our favor; Billy Bob and I felt like brothers. He has a quiet dedication that is similar to mine. The Teatro workshop was not built with *Sling Blade* in mind but the strangeness of the Teatro was perfect for my strange friend. Perhaps it was that premonitional force at work again, and it saw the future even if I couldn't.

Sling Blade became a contemporary classic; it won an Oscar, and Billy was catapulted to stardom. I keep in touch with Billy. We both miss the Teatro and fantasize about having another theater one day.

3

FLORIDA

I left a note on the steering wheel of my mother's car, explaining to her that I had to go. My best friend, Twig, and I had decided to hitchhike to Florida from Canada. Twig's brother Walt and their foster brother, Chris, had already left, and we were to meet them there. Twig and I hitchhiked across the Detroit border; eighteen-wheeler drivers sympathetic to two young traveling boys offered Twig and me transport. I was fifteen, Twig was fourteen.

Hitchhiking still had romance and dignity associated with it back then, perhaps because owning a car was not everybody's privilege. Mid-century generosity was still somewhat alive. The term "Good Samaritan" still had a position. A hitchhiker back then was viewed as searching and wayward, and not necessarily as a creep. Technology was on the rise, and North America was operating at the beginning of several media. To have a camera in your hand was still special and not commonplace. Not everybody had a TV, not everybody had a car, and consequently, there was a window of dynamic range available to the have-nots. There was plenty of time for acquisition, and you were not regarded to be second rate just because you weren't surrounded by status sundries. The maverick was not a bum. Looking at a beautiful continent through hopeful eyes had poetry and Jack Kerouac in it, not Charles Manson. Calculated cult murders and suicides had not happened yet. Magazine culture was not yet dominating all the senses; if you wanted to live life and see more, you stuck your thumb out and the road was your friend.

We made it all the way down to Florida, and I got a job at the IHOP in Hollywood Beach. Twig and I had met up with Walt and Chris, and everybody was broke, four Canadians living in one room, and me working at the IHOP to bring home the bacon. I literally brought home the bacon, also pancakes, home fries, and bread. I was the busboy, my finger was on the pulse. Good leftovers didn't get thrown in the garbage, they ended up in my backpack. The boys were always happy to see me after work. I was the hand that fed them.

We met some girls at the beach. They had a rich father, so they became our chauffeurs with the use of Daddy's car. The girls lived on a horse ranch on the outskirts of town. Consequently, I developed a keen interest in horseback riding. Their father was a six-foot-seven handsome John Wayne sort of guy, who tolerated our presence with a watchful eye. I could just imagine what was going on in his mind—better his girls in the hands of polite Canadian boys than some of the whacked-out locals. We had a sense of adventure and we weren't carrying guns. The girls were wild, and they supplied us with everything: transport, booze and drugs, lots of late-night fun. I suppose girls have always liked something about ramblers. How does a girl feel when she finally tames a rambler?

I got fired from the IHOP without pay when they realized I was Canadian with no American Social Security number. We were still broke, but our bellies were full. The foster brother,

Chris, never left Florida. Walt became a painter and moved to Belgium. I still see Twig regularly—he's a builder and art collector in Canada—and as for myself, I now have my U.S. work permit.

It wasn't too many years after that I got into motorcycles and began to feel the call of the open road once more. My first Harley-Davidson was a 1968 Sportster with a 1965 engine. The mismatch of frame to engine is always grounds for suspicion. My brother Bob and I had bought this bike from some heavy local bikers, who were likely unloading it cheap because it was hot. We gave the bikers eight hundred dollars cash and hauled the bike out of their basement without having ridden it. They gave it a kick in the basement, it started up okay, and that was good enough for us.

The bike was a bitch to start, and sometimes the only way to get it going was to tie a rope to the front forks and pull it with my mother's Chevy, Bob at the wheel, me on the bike. It was a magneto rig, which means no battery. The force of a kick or the turning of the back wheel provided a spark to the cylinders, much like an old-school generator that physically rubs on the front wheel of a bicycle to run the headlamp. There's a kind of genius to the concept, because you never have to rely on battery power. This technology was abandoned nonetheless and now all motorcycles have battery/electric start. I can remember pulling the Sportster with my mother's car to get it started in front of the license bureau to pass my motorcycle license test. The license bureau instructor rolled his eyes, and in the name of the raw bravado of two teenage brothers, he sympathetically granted me my license.

Bob and I had saved up a bit of cash, and we were now ready to buy a second bike. There it was, right in the front window—a brand-new red metal-flake Norton Commando. No electric start, a kicker with high compression. Both of these bikes were beasts, and if you weren't careful, they could backfire, throw you up in the air, and really hurt your leg. We had to master top dead center, which is a term that describes the optimum position of the two cylinders before you throw your full weight into the kick. A lot of bikers damage their knees from not being careful. You could think of this as a relative to those films you see of old prop plane ground operators, spinning the prop with their hands for the engine to then catch and ignite. Electric starters were beginning to come into fashion, but if you were a real biker, you still kicked.

By the time we were ready to roll across the continent, Bob and I had already lived our nine lives. My poor mother had put up with everything: delinquency, drugs, cosigning for bank loan qualification, the lower part of her house closed off to her. The experiments that happened in the basement were unspeakable; the only possible savior for her two sons was music and that recording studio. We closed the studio to accommodate this mad wintertime motorcycle adventure.

This was around the time of the Peter Fonda, Jack Nicholson, Dennis Hopper film *Easy Rider*. Motorcycle appreciation was in the air, and we were out to see what America had to offer to two wayward sons. I blew out the front tire of my Sportster doing ninety miles an hour outside London, Ontario. My brother watched me hit the ditch; he was riding behind me on the Norton. The blowout forced us to spend the night in a snowy field. A couple of sympathetic cops radioed to have some help sent to us for a tire replacement.

Having crossed the border at Detroit, Highway 75 took us through a bleak Ohio, and as we approached Kentucky and Tennessee, the snow started to melt and the vista became incredible: blue green pines cutting into forever-blue skies. Everybody we met along the way was kind. American idealism was on the rise.

Black ice was everywhere,
at every corner, but we didn't care.
Silver riding, silver nights, silverado.
The depth of the dream we fell in
Not for any tongue to speak in
Ah yes, it's all right to see
The light to eternal and
Silver riding, silver nights, Silverado.
The laughter would not quit;
it really felt like it was it.
The fever was so strong, the nights were never wrong.
Sweet empire times, before the bomb burned out the rye.
No worries came to mind, we walked through doors of time,
drunk on a silver moon, singin' out sweet our tune.
Silver nights with my brother, Silverado.

Two Canadian brothers at the peak of their curiosity, we couldn't wait to see what would happen over the next hill. My Fender Telecaster guitar was in my backpack in two pieces; I'd had to unbolt the neck. We rolled into Cape Kennedy and rented an old Airstream trailer for the night. The rent was cheap, and the trailer park woman was kind. We put our stuff in the trailer, and went into town to eat. When we got back, the walls of the trailer were crawling with cockroaches. We spent the night sleeping on the beach.

Bob and I found a better place the next day—an unfurnished apartment made of wood and built up on stilts, with an orange tree in the back. The oranges didn't look pretty on the outside, but they were delicious. The apartment had some leftover building materials underneath. A large disused roll of chicken wire was about to become the comfortable foundation to our new design: the chicken-wire bed. Our carpentry experience from the time spent living with my dad was about to be put to use. The frame of the bed was made of two-by-twos nailed together, with the chicken wire slung across the frame. The Chicken-Wire Hammock! Let's call George Foreman. My neck was pretty numb from the three-thousand-mile run on my rattling Sportster. It's still a little bit numb today.

The beach was nearby, and there was a cool scene going on there: blasting sound systems on the roofs of cars, all kind of hippies and renegades congregating for a music-driven good time. Julie was a wild child whose sunshine beauty caught my eye. My Sportster didn't have a backseat, so Julie had to sit on the fender as we rode through the ins and outs of Florida's balmy seaside nights.

I loved Julie, so I went to her house to meet her father. I don't think her father liked me or my motorcycle. He liked my jacket even less—I was wearing a military jacket with stripes on the shoulder. Apparently, more stripes than the old man had acquired through his entire military career. He did not allow me to leave the premises until I had removed these stripes, stitch by stitch, in his presence. I was not trying to insult the military; I just liked the jacket. My Canadian naïveté had deemed me not a potential son-in-law, so that was the end of the romance. I rattled the house's windows with the straight pipes of my 883. I never saw Julie again.

There was revolution in the air; the Vietnam War was being highly questioned. Protests had hit the streets, and American music was tainted by the event. "Fortunate Son" by Creedence Clearwater Revival addressed the issue of the sons of the rich carefully guarded by connection, bypassing being shipped off to Vietnam to be put at risk. Jimmy Hendrix had reduced or elevated the American national anthem to a dive-bomb, physiological experience. Four dead in Ohio, the military was gunning down white American youth. America went crazy. This was pretty much the turning point of America's involvement in Vietnam; no way was America gonna put up with college students getting shot on campus by the military. The senselessness of it all was knocking the wind out of the wide-eyed naïve spirit of America.

When brass shavings from fractured bushings started showing up in the oil of the crankcase of my Harley-Davidson, I knew the bike had only a few more miles left in it. The Harley packed it in on the exit ramp to Gainesville, Florida. This college town would become my home for the next seven months. The Norton Commando was still running fine, and so Bob rode back to Canada solo, and I moved into a large hippie house in Gainesville.

The house had a guy we called Wacko in it, a harmonica player from New York. Wacko had had trouble with drugs, and was recovering in this house of camaraderie. The rest of the residents were all students. I made a living by making sand-cast candles. Somebody before me at the house had built a candle-making operation in a little shed in the back. They had moved out, but all their equipment was still there, so I took over. My method of candle making involved creating an impression in the sand, and pouring hot wax into it. When the wax cooled down, the lump of sand roughly resembled the impression and with a small knife, I turned the lump into a beautiful sand sculpture. Part of the trick of course, was to accommodate the wick while the wax was still hot. My candles became more beautiful at every step. I experimented with different colors of dyes, and I became a popular local candle maker.

Music festivals were on the rise and Gainesville was about to be my first pop festival. I set up my candle display outside the event. The place was an outdoor sports stadium, capacity roughly ten thousand. To my surprise, the concertgoers bought all my candles. I was rich and I got to go to the show. Grand Funk Railroad was on stage when I walked in—a powerful trio with great vocals. The next act was Ian and Sylvia and the Great Speckled Bird. Ian and Sylvia sang beautifully; they were part of the country rock movement of the time, white trooper light dripping over Sylvia's white dress, her high, quivering folksinging accompanied by raindrop steel guitar notes. Little did I know that that would soon be me, playing steel guitar for Sylvia Tyson. There were not a lot of steel players around Toronto, and I still don't know if it was the power of my dreams or good old-fashioned word of mouth, but an invitation did come, and I did join Sylvia's band, and I did find myself at Maple Leaf Gardens in Toronto playing to ten thousand people. It was just like I remembered it in Gainesville—white trooper light dripping on Sylvia's white dress—but it was me next to her playing the raindrop steel.

The Allman Brothers from Macon, Georgia, had also crossed into my world. Their commitment had gotten under my skin. They were also part of the country rock and blues movement of the time. Timmy Thomas, from Florida, was another artist who touched me with his deeply soulful solo organ rendition of his song "Why Can't We Live Together." Appalachian melodies, whether I actually heard them or just felt them blowing through the evergreens of Tennessee and Kentucky, were also with me. These melodies, distant relatives of ancient Irish tunes, were part of the building of rock 'n' roll: Appalachian melodies pushed to the south, Mississippi and Louisiana slave chants pushed to the north, Texas swing pushed to the east, and rock 'n' roll was born. I was only a bystander in the evolution of this great music, but a small taste was all I needed to carry on with my music in the north.

My candle-making career came to an end when the students

from my hippie house took over the college campus in protest of the war in Vietnam. All kinds of FBI and narcotics agents started hanging around town. I unbolted the neck from my Telecaster guitar, put it in my backpack, and that was the end of Florida. I returned to Canada, fueled by the music I had heard.

4

SOUND PRESSURE

I've always loved thematic continuity in architecture, and I love it in records. The house that I stay in when I'm in Los Angeles is called Bella Vista. Built in 1929, Bella Vista has its name cast in the heavy iron of its commanding, swinging front gate. The metalworking hands of that time were dedicated, driven by a master aesthetic plan. The gothic floral ironwork of the gate shows up in different parts of the house, even in vestibules, connecting hallways and back bathrooms. It might take years to fully understand and digest the surprising details of the Bella Vista ironwork, but it means that the story unfolds over the course of time. This makes for longevity and lasting appeal. I like the records I make to have that thematic lasting potency.

Thematic continuity can be accomplished by simply having a few ground rules to operate by. For example, Eno's Ambient series records were built to provide atmosphere. They are reliably instrumental, mood-enhancing, and uninterruptive. The records were designed with the listener in mind; the listener is invited to be a member of the orchestra simply by being in the room of playback.

Every record should have ground rules that relate to the expectations of the artist. A ground rule that seems to work is to simply say, "We will make a record with what we have to work with." Five people in a room, no more. Five sounds, no more.

Expanding on available ingredients has always been part of my thing. Sometimes it's better to make more of an existing resource. On a recent Dobro guitar recording, I used the conventional microphone in front of the guitar but combined it with a version of the signal played through a spooky-sounding old Silvertone amplifier. The onboard tremolo and reverb provided the Dobro with a new dimension—let's call it the second dimension (the Dobro has a little electric guitar pickup). I had been after this multidimensional sound ever since I heard a cool old John Lee Hooker recording, with his vocal—bone dry—occupying center stage, his guitar clearly coming through an amp with tremolo and reverb, and then John Lee's third dimension: the sound of his foot stomping.

I've added a fourth dimension to this John Lee Hooker type of setup by introducing effects pedals—say a wah-wah, a distortion, or an envelope follower—to yet another guitar amplifier (optionally hidden in a side room, so as not to disturb John Lee). This little station of effects expression is controlled by me or another musical person involved in the project to perform sound-effects moves relative to the main guitar player's performance. All of these sounds are variations on the pure-source guitar performance.

On listening back to the recording, I can now introduce the fifth dimension. Much like the ironworkers who carried a theme through the beautiful Bella Vista, during this part of my work I am only repeating or enhancing or magnifying details of an already existing motif. I use sampling machines to catch fragments with the view of spinning them back into the song with a new texture.

This technique allows me to build an orchestra of sounds that relate to the song because they come from it. It's kind of interesting to think of the process as skin grafting or laboratory cell division from a donor or the magnification of a clothing motif, i.e., if the dress has a floral pattern, I would put a pocket on the dress with the same floral pattern, but blow it up twenty times bigger. Looking at the pocket would not tell you that it is the same pattern, but the tone and color would be relative. I've spent hours sampling, enhancing, and spinning these kinds of samples back into songs so that artists can have a beautiful custom sonic orchestra at their disposal. It has taken me twenty years to master this technique. The Zen of it appeals to me. The results are unique and original.

I had a little Gretsch Gadabout amplifier that I used to process Bob Dylan's vocals on *Time Out of Mind*. This processing was an extension of the same philosophy—take a sound that you already have and build a new dimension. In the case of *Time Out of Mind*, we wanted Bob's vocals to sound as great as the vocals on the rock 'n' roll records of the fifties. Other dimensions were added to his vocals by using some of my tried-and-true echoes à la Lee "Scratch" Perry (no reverb, only ever echo). Dimension on a song relates to "depth of field." As human beings we find comfort in depth: something that sounds far away is not an immediate danger; we are programmed to relax when prey is at a distance. Close sounds can be quiet and comforting, like the whispering of sweet nothings. A sweet nothing will still communicate over thunder, as long as the thunder is in the distance.

Back in 1987 in Dublin, my engineer and co-producer, Flood, and I wanted to build a new dimension for Larry Mullen's drums on "Bullet the Blue Sky" from U2's *The Joshua Tree*. Flood and I (mostly Flood) piped the acoustic recording of Larry's drum performance into a massive PA in the warehouse next door to the studio. The PA, as PAs do, made the drums sound "tankier" and more aggressive—it introduced a mid-range that the high-hat seemed to like. This new sonic emphasis on the high-hat made every hit more relevant. This is good, as Larry Mullen himself plays a mean high-hat. The inherent low-frequency punch of the PA also added a new level of excitement to the bass drum. The overall sensation was a chestier one. Our new drum sound had just crossed the line into physiological. This is where it gets abstract. This is where we record makers operate as illusionists.

I get this comment all the time: "You should have heard them live!"

People who hear a lot of bands live are addicted to the adrenaline and euphoria that is felt in the presence of stage charisma, mysterious light, and, most important to us record makers, sound pressure. Sound pressure is what you feel from the music when it is piped through a PA at 120 decibels. One hundred and twenty decibels starts to rattle the organs in your body. As your body responds to resonant frequencies, everything becomes exciting. The place is hot, the crowd is optimistic, and the moment is theatrical, but we record makers, we have to shut our eyes, because in the end we cannot depend on decibels, resonant frequencies of nightclubs, or charisma. We have to create the illusion of sound pressure. We have to make things sound loud even though they are being played back quietly on a little iPod. Oftentimes records sound cleaner than people would like, perhaps compression gets added by engineers to make things more exciting, but that doesn't give the same thrill.

The remiking of the drums through the PA worked for "Bullet the Blue Sky." The Gretsch Gadabout worked on Dylan's voice for *Time Out of Mind*, but those formulas may not apply to other projects. Ultimately it's a complete ad lib—it sure keeps me shaking in my boots—how to make records that have the feeling of sound pressure and still have body and fidelity intact.

5

THE NORTH

The circuit of the north had me living like a monk. I was cooking all my own food in an electric frying pan. I knew why I was out there—I had to save money.

I got to see plenty of the north of Ontario and Quebec—deep black lakes, granite formations cutting into the clean water of Canada. Pine trees reflecting, some fallen in the water, some pointing at the sky. Most people who visit the north are just vacationing. I worked my way there, and through there, playing in show bands.

This is not a glamorous chapter; it's a chapter of limbo that takes place before Eno, before any of the big albums. It's about putting in time because I had no better invitations to respond to, and so to pay the bills and to keep on playing music, I hit the road for a long time, making a hundred and fifty dollars a week. I've tried to block out this chapter, so I don't remember exactly how old I was, but for sure I remember my hundred and fifty dollars a week, sent home to my brother Bob to help keep the lights on in the recording studio.

A booking agent in Hamilton by the name of Sid kept twenty-five bands on the road, weaving them in and out of different towns in the north, playing one-week stints at hotels. Some of the stops were way up north, places like Kapuskasing, Thunder Bay, and Timmins. These places operated either because of mining or forestry. The clientele at those hotels was made up of workers—tough people all around, including the women. But we were also tough; you had to be to live the kind of life we were living. I kept my nose clean and to the grindstone.

All of my free time was spent playing the guitar. I had my steel on the road; I also played flute, tenor banjo, and of course regular electric guitar. My skills as a multi-instrumentalist were put to use on the show-band circuit. It had always been part of my thing: let's get Lanois because he plays a lot of different instruments. Even in my brief career playing in pit orchestras and full-size dance bands, this fact kept my name in the hat. My expertise on the Mini Moog, for example, made me valuable to the theater companies as an orchestra member. I supplied them with not only my regular music, but also the sounds of thunder, wind, and other special effects.

The theater companies got hooked on me, because I gave them more than they had bargained for—a full Foley department for the price of one guitar player. The Mini Moog was the beginning of the synthesizer becoming a common and available musical instrument; previously, synthesizers had lived in the electronic music departments of colleges, viewed as a relative of musique concrète. Further back, the Theremin, the first synthesizer ever, had reared its head as the solo operatic spooky, haunting voice heard in many early horror films. The Theremin, with a sine wave at its core, had only two controls: volume and pitch. The right hand went over an antenna to control volume, and the left hand over the other antenna to control pitch.

The Mini Moog synthesizer was similar to the Theremin,

except rather than having one sound source, it had two. It also had tonal variety. The Theremin had the sound of a female opera singer, but the Mini Moog went into the reeds section. You could get saxophone and bassoon sounds out of it. I became obsessed with the Mini Moog—I consider it the most exciting instrument of its time. But as advanced as it was, the Mini Moog had its limitations. Essentially a monophonic instrument, it didn't offer quick switching from one sound to another. I kept the parameter settings for my homemade sounds on diagrammed sheets of paper, essentially drawings of the front panel of the Moog.

As the pit orchestra performed the music for the play, I frantically set all the controls of the Mini Moog to ready myself for my next cue. In any given play, I might have twenty cues. Once cue number 8 had gone by (say, the sound of rain), I had to change all my settings to get ready for cue number 9 (which might be the sound of a stampede).

The electronic music explosion ran in tandem with the psychedelic music explosion. The pendulum swung wide—from Sly and the Family Stone playing down the street at the Town Hall, to Frank Zappa at the Rockpile in Toronto, to the psychedelic electronic music installation at the CNE (Canadian National Exhibition), complete with a two-hundred-speaker installation by the great Toronto equipment company Traynor. The Traynor installation still blows my mind today. A ten-thousand-square-foot room with two hundred speakers hanging from the ceiling, four feet above the heads of a thick crowd of psychedelic hopefuls. The lighting was the typical psychedelic lighting of the sixties, but the layout of the overhead speaker system was timeless; I can't think of a design that betters it. The only performers since that I've seen come close to using this idea are those of Cirque du Soleil. They have a center cluster of speakers that provides the same sound to all members of the audience by pointing a speaker evenly to every seating position in the room. But the CNE system was so much more: Have you ever been in a room with three thousand people in it, where every person gets to enjoy the sound within ten feet of a speaker?

I've already spoken of my disappointment with the usual front-speaker stacks in clubs. This incredible CNE system had no clutter on the floor, no visible wires, and sounded fantastic. The pulsing electronic music pouring out of two hundred Traynor speakers made the electro experience a physical one. People were touched by the sounds. Perhaps Traynor had found the resonant frequency of flesh and bone, or, better yet, serotonin. Imagine a future generation of eventgoers high on resonant frequency, no hangover. I've been wanting to reproduce it ever since.

The synthesizer movement of the sixties was all part of a musical cultural revolution. Check out Walter Carlos's *Switched On Bach*, and then Stevie Wonder, of course, when the synthesizer went polyphonic. Stevie Wonder's seventies masterpieces are dominated by these polyphonic sounds. The music instrument company Yamaha brought out a great polyphonic synthesizer—the CS-80. Eno and I used the CS-80 as the workhorse for many ambient recordings. "An Ending Ascent," on *Apollo*, is not only a fine example of Eno's genius, but also a representation of the wonderful CS-80 sound.

The northern Canada hotel gigs included accommodation. These funky old places oftentimes had the toilet down the hall, like in rooming houses. I can remember a big old rope, coiled up, anchored on the floor of my hotel room in Sturgeon Falls. This was the fire escape. If a fire broke out, the idea was to smash the window if you couldn't open it, throw the rope out the window, and climb down four stories to the ground. (It sounds archaic, but the more I think about it, the more the idea appeals to me these days. Some high-tech version of this might well apply to fire-escape design for contemporary high-rise buildings. To my knowledge, there is no "out the window" fire escape ever talked about in high-rise buildings, but I wouldn't want to depend on an elevator or an inner staircase if a burning building was full of smoke. If a window cleaner can dangle on a wire twenty-eight floors up, why can't a potential burn victim?)

Our agent, Sid, promised variety to hotel owners, and so each band had to have its own shtick. We traveled with a female impersonator named Ricky Day, a great old-school entertainer. It was pretty much Ricky's show. Ricky could really work the audience, handle any kind of heckling situation, outwit and quell the noisiest goofball in the crowd. The guys in the band were all young and good-looking, so that helped to bring in the female clientele. The male clientele, they showed up to see the stripper action in our show, the Delightful Delilah.

Ricky Day did a few numbers mixed in with comedy; then our singer was introduced. She did three numbers with the band before the big moment—Delightful Delilah! After being stuck in a nickel mine all week, a northern Canadian worker got to watch the Beautiful and Talented Delilah strip off her clothes and take a bath on stage. This embarrassingly low-grade entertainment unit was my family for a good long time.

Delilah had to leave after she accidentally sprayed hairspray in her eye; the poor girl's eye was really messed up. Sid sent us a replacement: Miss Montego, a very funny Jamaican woman with massive breasts—I mean size 54 quadruple E, something crazy. Business shot up; we became Sid's top band and I got worked into the act. Montego had apparently chosen me as the cute guitar player whose face she gyrated her breasts into. The lumberjacks shrieked and wahooed in envy, practically starting a riot every night. Montego then tasseled her nipples with tampons dipped in lighter fluid, and proceeded to light them on fire. This really brought the house down. Our lighting director (doubling as bass player) killed the lights on cue, as Montego wildly maneuvered her breasts, spinning the tampon tassels in one direction, and then the other, and then the real showstopper—one breast one way, the other breast the other way, all to a Gene Krupa drumbeat. The place went nuts, all kinds of drunken miners and lumberjacks falling down at the drool trough. It was like a bad dream, something out of the Old West.

Sid kept us moving. Every Saturday night after packing up our equipment, we received Sid's travel instructions to the next stop. This merry-go-round that Sid had invented was my limbo for a couple of years. The only saving grace was my capacity to dream. I couldn't wait to get back to the recording studio. This northern circuit was not providing me with any window of opportunity.

Perhaps Sid had been sent to me as penance for delinquency. Ah, the Dark Age, and my poor mother. What did she ever do to deserve what I did? I was different. A French Canadian in an Anglo burb, maybe it's as simple as that. But my mother was a fighter, and so was I.

Flashback to grade eight, elementary school. My gang and I were not liked by the principal; we pretty much ran the schoolyard. We even dictated the kinds of clothes that students wore: no brown socks. If you wore brown socks, you qualified for a dunking in the open mouth of the underground spring, at the bottom of the schoolyard field, at the edge of the woods. On hearing about a recent dunking, the principal called me into his office.

This was still the time of the strap, but this called for a more serious punishment. The school principal bypassed the strap and hit me straight in the face with hands and fists. I left the office bleeding at the mouth. The other guys in the gang got the same treatment.

I knew where the principal lived; my mind started building a plan for retaliation. That weekend, in the night, I filled two large cans (say five gallons each) with gasoline and made my way to the principal's house, a one-mile journey through ravines and back routes, so as not to be seen. I poured the entire contents of the cans around the principal's house and dropped a match. The whole neighborhood lit up in orange flame with black smoke. I ran for it, feeling that the principal and I were now back to even, a blank canvas. The cops picked me up the next day. I was real lucky, in fact, because the principal and his family were not in the house at the time of explosion. The house didn't burn down, because it was made of brick, but the paint on the windows and doors got pretty messed up, and the trees and bushes didn't do so well either.

What a great guy: the principal didn't press charges, and I agreed to have the house repainted and replace all his burnt bushes. This started my career in the gardening business. I got a job at the local nursery to make some cash and to have access to better prices on bushes. At this point, I was still delivering the paper in the mornings, so I worked at the garden center after school.

The place was run by a European woman who made me lift whole trees, roots balled up in burlap, really heavy. I lifted them into the trunks of customers' cars or I carried them off trucks for planting in the back of the nursery. It was hard labor. Once I had enough money to deal with the damage to the principal's house, I jumped the garden center fence and walked to the nearby diner. I ordered French fries and gravy, a cherry Coke, dialed up "Wipe

Out" by the Surfaris on the deep bass jukebox, and never looked back. That was the end of my gardening career.

Not far from the diner was the bowling alley, complete with a nice lunch counter and pool hall downstairs. This place was viewed as a bad-boy hangout, not a place for a kid, but I didn't care. I had a few friends that were much older than me. They had already quit school and drove customized hot rods.

The custom car scene was big at the time. A young man was a real man only if he knew his cars. If you could boast a hand-polished intake manifold, increasing "fuel to spark" efficiency, if you could boast nine coats of hand-rubbed lacquer, if you had managed to increase the power of your engine by adding a few horses to the already ridiculous horsepower rating of one of these Detroit City big-blocks—then you were a man. Cruising with your girl, with "no particular place to go"; purple dash lights; Hurst shifter, custom black ceramic shifter ball in the heat of your palm; Booker T. and the MG's "Green Onions" comin' at you from a one-point-source coaxial oval-shaped Jensen speaker; whipping down the escarpment into dead man's curve. Backcountry concession road, midnight daredevil racetrack. Two cars half a mile apart, one set of headlights one way, another set of headlights the other way—the race would start. Foot to the floor, the big-blocks roared. This greaseball version of medieval knights jousting was essentially a game of chicken. At redline r.p.m., the clutch popped, and the race began. This is where it got intense: two young men purposely screaming their engines into a full head-on collision. Who would be the first to get out of the way? That was the game. Whoever chickened out first lost the race.

The Lanois garage had pretty much been turned into a car-customizing shop by my brother Bob. My mother's 1966 Chevy Belair, 283 under the hood, two-speed automatic, Positraction rear end, became the neighborhood curiosity, with its Bob Lanois custom sound system. The rear speaker addition boasted a nice, deep sounding spring reverb system. Adding reverb to the a.m. radio broadcasts made our Chevy the talk of the street.

There was a musical merge going on at this point in time in North America, forces coming in from varied sources. You can think of it as a boiling point. Gospel music had swung all the way from the church to the top of the charts—Aretha Franklin, Sam Cooke, and Cissy Houston went from church singers to household names. The recording studio had evolved from a place of documentation to a place of innovation. Films like *Easy Rider* and later *Apocalypse Now* gave classic orchestral film scoring a new companion: rock 'n' roll. Hells Angels culture, hippie culture, the Detroit big-block had not been yet tamed by practicality, high gas prices, or feminism.

Music culture had not yet oversaturated itself. It was hard to fool a listener, so you had to be great. If you couldn't play, you couldn't get a foot in the door. Ravi Shankar could play, Jimi Hendrix could play, the Beach Boys could sing, Bob Dylan could write, Neil Young had his thing down, and the Beatles were not too shabby. There seemed to be no end in sight to the potential that we felt all around us, of space travel mixed with steamy nights of rock 'n' roll and hot-rod culture.

My brother Bob went from understanding the workings of a car engine to understanding the signal path of the electronics used in our studio experiments. For years my mother's basement was littered with breadboards. *Breadboard* is an electronics term used to describe a work in progress, essentially an open-faced version of the invention without a casing around it. The open face makes it easy to quickly try modifications by changing the values of components.

Understanding a chain of events from top to bottom requires

a lot of wisdom. Troubleshooting requires cool—you gotta be chilled to fully decipher a sequence of events from source to end. This is why young people are not surgeons. A surgeon will take symptoms into consideration that life and professional experience have shown him, but he has the entire signal path laid out in his head. The earlier you start understanding signal paths, the better chance you have at being a surgeon. The electronic world is the same, and my brother was the best. His understanding of the past made him cool enough under pressure to deal with the symptom, the inconvenient problem in the present.

But what about the future? This is where Bob and I are like twins; we both always look to the future. We have always operated by "feel," even when coming up with designs. My brother is an interesting cat, because he feels music deeply. His inventions for the studio always had a foot in the future because they were built to optimize productivity, for ease of ergonomic operation, and ultimately to maximize "feel." Our parallel dedications to detail, musical for me, electronic for my brother, meant that we always rode in tandem, whether we were cruising on motorcycles or building records.

The recording studio in my mother's basement boasted many Bob Lanois in-house electronic inventions—in no way was this a "straight out of the box" recording service. We wanted a distinct sound, like Motown in Detroit or Sun Studio in Memphis had. It wasn't hard to locate our window of opportunity. The other recording studios in the region offered a blank generic service, and so we went the other way. Pretty early on, Bob and I started collecting unique musical instruments. A band could show up at our studio and not even bring any of their own stuff. We had it all—a variety of drums, my personal guitar collection, a finely tuned in-house bass sound, pianos and keyboards already miked up, ready to go, hand-picked microphones plugged in, already set up with a good sound. We even had the sounds ready—the best Hammond B-3, unorthodox custom sound effects chains and a prepatched, instant sound, instant karma, in-house radio transmitter, for purposes of broadcasting mixes to the car radio. A client could drive around the block in his car to check the balance of a mix.

All these techniques were building blocks in a growing mythology. The word was out, Bob and I were doing something different. We even had in-house musicians, guys who could really play. Eddie Roth, for example, who worked for us since the basement days as a staff writer, was the best keyboard player around, a genius organist and composer, and an electronics wizard on top of all that. Eddie was addicted to coffee and cigarettes—this guy could outmarathon anybody. He had played with Rick James and everybody, and was always happy to accommodate a request to play a spontaneous overdub. The Lanois brothers didn't want to be generic; we wanted to have our own sound. This simple philosophy has been with me ever since.

Because Bob spoke the car lingo, he was part of that club of true customizers. I only ever stood on the outside. These guys, still hanging on to fifties values, knew the ins and outs of pool-hall and nightclub life, and I hung on their stories about the hot steamy nights of the summertime beach resorts, the dance-hall culture, places like Port Dover, Sauble Beach, and Grand Bend. Later on I had a chance to play these summer rock 'n' roll hangouts, in a six-piece soul band with my best friend, Bob Doidge.

We didn't expect the band to make money; we were happy playing for the love of music. Our singer, Wayne, was a native from the Six Nations reserve, with an incredible voice and charisma, a powerhouse sweet, musclebound, skinny-legged, sharp-suit-wearing descendant of Joe Tex. Our repertoire developed in the basement of my girlfriend Karen's father's farmhouse, way out in Copetown, where the Doidge and I would hitchhike, him blowing his trumpet into the sky and me waving my arms and ranting about dreams and places to go. Nothing could stop us, especially with the Doidge's talent; he could play "Flight of the Bumble Bee" on his Olds Mendez trumpet when he was only five years old. I felt blessed to be in the company of his genius. The hitchhiking trip sometimes took hours, but we didn't care. "Silver riding, silver nights, Silverado."

Murray, the father of my girlfriend Karen, filled the role of my missing father. Al Gore would have liked to meet Murray, back then. A fifth-generation farmer born in the house that we were rehearsing in, Murray knew plenty about climate change; the pond down the hill, for example, didn't freeze over anymore, the very pond that Murray had skated on when he was small. The intelligence of Murray burned through me. He could stand on that TH&B (Toronto, Hamilton, and Buffalo) railway bridge and tell you exactly what was going on with the economy, relative to the freight train action: Massey Ferguson farming equipment heading south, Detroit automobile industry cars coming north. Murray could tell you if the harvest had been good; he could smell the difference between two batches of diesel fuel, and he could tell you by the smell of the diesel if the train had fueled up in Canada or Stateside. The struggling, roaring sound of an engine trying to creep its way up the Niagara Escarpment would tell Murray, even when he was lying in bed, what kind of frost the Canadian National diesel engines were fighting against on that cold Canadian winter morning.

Karen's brother Brian, who played rhythm in the soul band, was my freight-train-hopping friend, who pushed my ass up into an empty boxcar on many occasions when the struggling CN diesels provided the opportunity, as they chugged up the escarpment by Murray's house, doing ten miles an hour. Once the diesel had pulled its cargo past the long grade, it had won the battle and it was smooth sailing all the way to Sault St. Marie. Two teenagers in a boxcar, wondering if the train was ever going to stop. Karen herself was beautiful and amazing, and if arranged marriage had been part of our culture, I would have been happy if Murray had chosen me to be her lifelong.

"Mercy! Mercy! Mercy!" rang up the stairs from the Murray Bonham house. The basement was a storage area meant for preserves, but we didn't care that we were standing on a dirt floor. We were just happy to be playing music, to be living off the sweat of soul and rock 'n' roll. As I think about it now, how remarkable it was: that the power of Otis Redding, Sam and Dave, Joe Tex, James Brown, and Sam Cooke could have gotten under the skins of six white kids in a basement in Copetown, Ontario.

The Grand Bend dance hall was a beauty. It was essentially a big-band-era construction, all made of wood, with very large booths; each could fit sixteen people. The stage was massive, built to accommodate full-size bands. Summer fair ground rides across the parking lot provided a romantic dim neon light to lovers in the grass. You could hear it in the wind, "under the boardwalk," "only the lonely," "two silhouettes on the shade," "Sleepwalk" by Santo and Johnny, "Boom boom boom boom . . . oohoohoohooh white lightning!" All the fantastic melting-pot music of that era had slowly but surely reached the great white north.

At the dance hall, a young man's bravado was his friend—to chance a walk across the dance floor, to hold out a hand to a girl whom he liked, to pull her onto the floor, to risk her saying no—cheek to cheek, sweat mixed with makeup and perfume. The Doidge would be screeching on his trumpet, me on my white

Strat, our conductor, Wayne the Indian, screaming at the top of his lungs—a better night than any night could ever be. That's where the older custom-car greaseballs brought their stories back from.

Tony, one of the hometown custom-car heroes, told me about a pinsetting job that I might be able to get at the bowling alley, and put in a word for me. The Chinese owner turned a blind eye to my being too young, and said okay, five pins, one lane at a time. I sat on top of the rail at the end of the lane just above the pins and waited for the bowler to smash them down. If a strike didn't happen, I jumped down and got rid of the fallen ones, to ready the lane for the next throw. When I got better, they gave me two lanes to work at a time. Some of the pinsetters had been there for years; they had all kinds of scars on their faces from the flying pins.

I loved everything about this job. The shiny lacquered bird's-eye-maple bowling lanes reminded me of the maple slab of my Fender Telecaster. The little markings on the bowling alley were like the recessed markings on the neck of my guitar. The jukebox was pumping, the girls were hot, and I could eat at the lunch counter. It was all pure rock 'n' roll, plus they were paying me money. I was hooked on work, and I realized something simple then: skill was an automatic ticket to any interesting scene. I made a decision that I would never ask for anything from the table, I would always bring something instead.

My pinsetting career came to an end when the owner brought in an automated system. Down the road was the butcher shop, so I took a job there as the hamburger grinder. The only hard part about grinding hamburger is that you have to be standing in the meat cooler to do it; otherwise it's pretty simple. All the shop's extra trimmings of meat, fat, and scraps got dumped in a huge barrel, whose contents I would lift out and pour into a massive tray. At the end of the tray was a large open mouth, which led to the grinding blades of the burger maker. The machine spat out a soft, spaghetti-like pulp, which my hands guided onto yet another tray for display at the counter. The only mysterious part of the process was the "goof." The butcher-shop man had made it clear that I shouldn't worry my pretty little head about it, and so, no questions asked, I would sprinkle an entire fist of white powder "goof" (like powdered sugar on a cake) over the pinky white mounds of ground meat to watch them magically turn bright blood red in twenty minutes. This butcher shop boasted the best burger meat in town, even if aided considerably by red dye number 3.

The butcher shop taught me the fundamentals of business. The stuff gets delivered in the back, and you sell it out the front. If what you sell it for at the front is more than what you paid for it in the back, and the cost of your staff and keeping the lights on doesn't kill you . . . then you're floating. You're in business.

I fell in love with the cashier, an older woman—age seventeen. We both worked at the butcher shop after school. There was a makeshift dressing room in the back of the shop where the cashier used to change into her work outfit. My curiosity was certainly fueled by the changing-room action in the back, but I kept my feelings to myself. A small crack in the door of the dressing room could easily have made a thirteen-year-old hamburger grinder into a Peeping Tom.

That meat cooler eventually made me sick, and I began to think about how I could make money and be outside at the same time. There were rumblings of a job opportunity at the local golf course. If you managed to work your way up through the ranks of caddying, you could make a lot of bucks. It all sounded better than the meat cooler. I moved on to the golf course, and that was the end of the butcher business.

Caddying was not everything I'd hoped it would be. My waterlogged Hush Puppies felt pretty bad on my feet after eighteen holes in the morning dew. Golfers didn't use motorized golf carts much back then; walking the eighteen holes was just as important as playing them. I learned the lingo and caught on to golfing and its rules pretty quickly. The club, however, had a built-in snottiness; its members were the rich or the descendants of important people, and this might very well be the place where I first felt racism. My complexion was especially dark in those days, and golf here was dominated by a white, largely Scottish presence. If you were French Canadian like me, or Native, or Italian, or Portuguese, or, God forbid, black, this place was not very welcoming. *It took a while, but all that has changed—Otis Redding could sing better than everybody, James Brown was the funkiest man on the planet, no great white hope lasted long in front of Muhammad Ali, and then the cherry on the cake—Tiger Woods kicked everybody's ass, including Scottish ass, at golf.*

My uncle Paul slipped me a few of his old clubs, and that was the beginning of my golfing career. My mother's house was not far from the course. At the dead end of our street, there was a wooded access to the eighth hole. Hiding in the woods, my brother and I could easily spot a window of opportunity, as a cluster of golfers moved on to the ninth. This is where I made my hole in one. I smacked the ball with a 5 iron; it soared over the eighth—a par three with a pond—hit the green, and bounced in the cup. I ran back into the woods with my brother: we could see golfers coming on to the seventh.

Bob and I wanted to improve our putting. We decided that

making our own green in our mother's backyard was the way to do it. The season was already half gone, so it would have taken too long to grow the grass properly. So late one night, we rolled a wheelbarrow to the green of the seventh hole, and with good sharp knives in hand, we carefully cut and lifted a fifteen-by-fifteen-foot patch of it. The predug empty dirt patch in my mother's yard was soon covered with the most exquisite blue-green sod donated by our local golf club. Several back-and-forth trips completed the transplant, and then as the finale, we added the cup and the flagpole. My mother was mystified by the sudden green in her yard, but at this point she had pretty much lost control of her boys. She rolled her eyes and went to work. The relocation of the seventh is impressive on a level of determination, but the dishonesty still hurts.

Long drives in the north can make you forget that people even exist. The ancient landscapes are timeless. Our old Bell telephone van rattled on the highway to North Bay, a thick vibe in the air because our singer was quitting the band. North Bay was to be her last week. She couldn't handle hotel existence, and the cold trips between cities, traveling in a stuffy van, finally pushed her back east to her mom. Sid sent us two new singers: Fran Ceslo and Noreen Mullen.

Fran was a powerhouse singer, and Noreen was her impeccably accurate harmony singer. The level of quality in the vocal department shot up, and Fran, Noreen, and I worked up a lot of cool harmonies. Now, not only did we have Miss Montego, we had the best harmony singing in the entire Sid roster. Fran would turn around with daggers in her eyes if I sang out of tune. I have a tendency to sing sharp, and I have to say that she was a hell of an Italian auto-pitch corrector. One glare from Fran was enough to set me straight for the rest of the night.

Our band got so good that Sid booked us into the Brown Derby on Yonge Street in Toronto. The Derby was the best old-school entertainment club in Toronto. It wasn't enough to play a string of songs; you had to have a show. The club boasted a connection with Las Vegas, and come to think of it, we might even have been billed as "Direct from Las Vegas." The Derby was next door to Le Coq d'Or, which was the Toronto crossroads for traveling blues artists. I went to see Muddy Waters there. In between the Brown Derby sets, I would slip into Le Coq d'Or and hear frighteningly deep blues music.

The blues music of the Coq resonated all the way back to the cotton fields. This music had a search for freedom resonating from the core of its bones. The Edison, next door, featured country music. That's where I first heard Bob Lucier, my French Canadian steel guitar teacher-to-be.

To maximize my sleep, I lived in Toronto at the bass player's house. It made it easier on me because we never got out of the Derby till three in the morning, and so my friend let me use his couch. This was an interesting time for Toronto. Two years later all those cool clubs on Yonge Street were knocked down to build a shopping mall. It was not long after all this that I decided to leave the Toronto area, partly due to a work invitation in Europe, but mostly because I wasn't hearing any music in Toronto that satisfied my appetite for soul. Soul music is music that rises up from inside you because it has to. It operates outside the restrictions and preconceptions of the music business.

By the time of the Brown Derby, our band had added a great singer named John Lovet. Lovet was a funk man, and he pushed the repertoire to a rhythmic place I had not known before. All the northern trudging began to make some kind of sense, as my funk guitar chops grew quickly. A guitar style that I had begun as a flirtation was now something that belonged to me. Lovet himself was a great funk guitar player, a crazy, obsessive Iggy Pop sort of character—all muscle, steak, and coffee. Late nights, he worked on his dance moves while I worked on my funk rhythms; we never stopped, we just did the funk. I believe my time with Lovet was like a college course preparing me for my later work with the Neville Brothers. I studied the funk like a student studies anthropology; the ghosts of Jimmy Nolan, Leo Nocentelli, and John Lovet pushed me to a new level of knowledge about rhythm.

Without exposing all the intimate details, I have to admit that the drug culture of the time did swallow me up for a while. When I just about got shot in the face by a paranoid speed freak holding a hunting rifle, I decided that this volatile drug world could operate without Danny Lanois. Music, my angel savior, came down to see me one more time and whispered: The long road may make you sweat, but the short road will make you bleed.

When our show band disintegrated, everybody went their own ways. I decided to hook up with my old friend Curlie for my next chapter of live performances. We had grown up together; he was the best singer in our neighborhood. Curlie knew hundreds of songs. His capacity to remember lyrics and musical details still impresses me today. We used to wave our arms around in the basement of my mother's house, pretending to be orchestra conductors. His imagination was even crazier than mine. Curlie was really good with harmonies, and his encouragement has a lot to do with the fact that I am singing at all today.

Curlie lived in a tree house and read Henry David Thoreau. His father was the village doctor, my doctor, in fact. The annual checkup never amounted to much, other than being drilled by Curlie's dad about who was taking drugs in our circle of friends. Curlie's tree house overlooked the Speed River in Cambridge, Ontario. The river bend by the tree house was a landing point for the great blue heron. This bird, with its prehistoric beauty, made a lasting impression on my brain.

Ey Bebette, danse avec moi
Ce soir au fais do-do
Danse avec moi, bebette
Under the stormy sky
I hear the whippoorwill cry
I see the blue heron fly over sugar hill snowy white
big blue siren in the night
Come with me, hey Bebette
Under the stormy sky
My heart is sad to leave sugar town
Goodbye sugar hill on this stormy night

Curlie and I were a duo. Having just two of us helped to avoid problems with band politics. Our new streamlined operation was about to hit the road in response to an invitation to tour Bobby Orr's pizza chain. Bobby Orr, one of our most famous Canadian hockey players, had eight pizza shops sprinkled around Ontario. Curlie and I had gotten the job directly from the Bobby Orr office, and so there was no agent to pay, no more Sid.

I strapped my homemade PA on the roof of Curlie's tiny Austin Mini 850, and off we went. It must have been quite a sight. The 850 rolling down the highway with something bigger than itself on its back, with a Wurlitzer electric piano, two banjos (tenor and five-string), steel guitar, acoustic and electric guitars, amps and accessories crammed inside. The Bobby Orr pizza tour paid good money. Curlie was great with the crowd, and the fact remains: we sounded fantastic together. Curlie's deep velvet voice kept the girls coming back, and where the girls are, the boys will follow.

During this time period I was also studying with Tony Braden. There was nothing rock 'n' roll about Tony. He was an old-school big-band guitarist who a lot of players in the area had studied with. Once a week, I drove to Toronto to study the structure of harmony and arrangement of music. Tony taught me the shapes of chords, and how a particular inversion of a chord could be more harmonious to a melody than another. A D chord on a guitar can be played in many positions. A beginner, someone playing a common folk song like "Red River Valley," would likely play the D chord in its first position, and it would sound great. However, as compositions and melodies become more complex, the hand may do better to use a different position. A D chord will usually have the D note in the bottom as its fundamental, but adding the third in the bass, which in the case of the D chord is F-sharp, creates a rising effect. It is still just a D chord, but has a different feeling. This new, second-position D chord, with the F-sharp in the bass, creates a feeling of optimism and opens the doorway to the fourth, which in the key of D will be the G chord.

You can hear what I'm talking about in U2's song "In a Little While," which uses this "third in the bass" Tony Braden trick. You can also hear it in Marvin Gaye's "Sexual Healing." Tony Braden might have been from another generation, but he was very musical and patient, and much like the hands of the great Garth Hudson, Tony's hands held secrets that rock 'n' roll didn't know. I took the Tony Braden teachings back to Hamilton with me every week and passed on whatever I could of it to the kids I was teaching myself, in the front room of my mother's house, three nights a week. The cycle of information is interesting to me.

When you have to teach somebody something, you become a better learner.

Business boomed and so it was time for a bigger vehicle. Curlie and I traded in the 850 for a nice Ford cargo van. We couldn't believe how good the deal was. The 850 plus five hundred bucks got us the van . . . but there was a catch. The used-car dealer said we had to take the cargo that was already in the back of the van. The cargo just looked like a big pile of leaves and shrubbery, and so we agreed, and drove off into a cold Ontario night.

The next morning was hot and sunny. We loaded up our musical equipment on top of the heap of shrubbery. Twenty minutes out of town, the van started to smell really bad. Curlie pulled over, and on close inspection, the used-car salesman had gotten the better part of the deal. The layer of shrubbery was in fact a thin cosmetic disguise to a ton of human waste. The Ford cargo van had apparently been the dumping site for the contents of several portable toilets. When a deal is too good to be true, it probably is.

The Bobby Orr pizza tour ended, and as we drove into Hamilton at sunrise, the cargo van packed it in. The smoke signals rising up from the overheated burned-out engine was a sign that I had had enough. I swore to be dedicated to my recording studio from there on.

6

WAIST DEEP IN TWO-INCH TAPE

I wish I had a snapshot of myself in 1986 standing in Peter Gabriel's control room after having been up all night editing Robbie Robertson's "Sweet Fire of Love." This was a track we had cut at Adam Clayton's house, the house where we had worked on *The Joshua Tree* back in Dublin. U2 had kindly agreed not only to host Robbie's visit to their studio, but also to be Robbie's band for a couple of songs. I was now standing in Peter's room with two-inch tape up to my waist after frantically editing together a bunch of takes to make sense of the backing track. Perhaps Larry Mullen had been right about cutting one more take. We hadn't, and I was paying the price. Just one slippery bar in the performance meant that I had to create a Band-Aid to repair it. This meant either making twenty-four-track copies of good bars to be cut back into the multi, or finding the replacement bar from some other take. In the morning Robbie walked in, worried that I looked sick, and in fact I was; sick like the many times before. It was the familiar "up all night" feeling; fighting for a track, I was like a guy trying to manicure a sandy beach to look pretty after a hurricane.

The sick "up all night" feeling never gets talked about in my line of work, because it doesn't hold any anecdotes. You're there alone, knowing that the progress of the session is hinging on your ability to raise the work to the next level of stability. Like being a dressmaker with the most beautiful design, realizing that he is just a bit short of material. The Robbie Robertson record had taken longer than expected, so there I was in the middle of making U2's *The Joshua Tree*, trying to also finish Robbie's work. Bringing the Robbie record to Europe was my way of making Robbie, a fellow Canadian, feel connected with the rest of what was going on workwise in my life; and I also felt it would be good for Robbie's record to have some European rock 'n' roll flavors.

Peter Gabriel let us use his place in the West Country of England for a few days and also agreed to help out on a song for Robbie called "Broken Arrow." I was no stranger to Peter's studio. It had been my home for a year during the making of his *So* album. *So* had just gone through the roof, playing on radio everywhere. The single "Sledgehammer" was number 1 in America. MTV played the song's innovative video on an endless loop, catapulting Peter to a new level of stardom. But there I was, considered to be one of the top record producers in the world, waist deep in two-inch tape, sick, up all night, trying to make sense of all these pieces of tape, china-marked with arrows and instructions about which way to glue them all back together. I felt like some specialist surgeon, unraveling cancerous intestines, cutting out the bad parts, and sticking it all together again to give somebody back their life. If there was an Olympic team for tape editing, I would have been on it. I had reached some bizarre level of madness with a razor blade, like those kids you see on spelling-contest shows; you couldn't stump me. You didn't even have to feed me. I was living off the fumes from the tape. I was sleeping, eating, dreaming tape. I had become a piece of tape. The sheer stamina alone was enough to justify an honorary Ph.D.

The year spent with Peter Gabriel for the making of *So* had been good. I loved him like a brother. I fought for him at every bend in the road. Peter had been introduced to my work by his friend David Rhodes, who loved the Harold Budd records I had worked on with Eno. Peter's initial invitation was for me to produce a soundtrack for an Alan Parker film called *Birdie*. The film told the story of a young American soldier (featuring a young Nicolas Cage), who returns from Vietnam shell-shocked and permanently perching like a bird. The soundtrack had gone well and Peter invited me to stay on and work on his singing record *So*. Peter's studio was a converted cattle barn. The control room was not much to look at, but it sounded great and the view was magnificent. It was just outside Bath, and the running grassy hills, often garnished with a burst of sudden biblical sunshine, took my breath away. Peter was in a good place with his ideas, and nothing meant more to me than to harness them all together for my new friend.

There have been times on meeting someone when I have felt I have known them from the past. When I first arrived at Peter Gabriel's and saw him at a distance, I felt I had met him before. He had the eyes of a relative, a bit like my cousin Michel who I spent summers with in rural Quebec. Michel used to shout at me, "Rame, Dan! Rame, Dan!" which means "Row the boat, Dan! Row the boat, Dan!" as we floated over black lakes, seeking out a choice *bouleau* (birch) for the building of a tree house. Two boys on the black water—no life jackets, no parental eyes, no questions about our motives, just us. When I saw Peter, I trusted my feelings, and accepted that I was working with a relative. We didn't know what we were about to do, but I knew that Peter was made of good. That was enough for me to go on.

The strange ability that I have to focus is hard to understand, even by me. I'm not saying this to honk my own horn; I'm saying it because it's a psychological curiosity. I don't even know if intelligence can be brought into the equation. During this chapter of my work, I never had a chance to think about the broader picture. The obsessive condition of my brain would have been a study in itself. I wouldn't wish it upon anyone. It was a very hard time, a very successful time—it hurts to think about it.

As I look through my old workbooks, I sense the level of obsession I had reached. The intricate details covering every nuance of song arrangements border on forensic. The planned psychological maneuvers to steer Peter in a certain direction, the pain I felt when it was not going well—I saw every problem as a personal obstacle to knock down. Now that I can stand back, I can see that the technique used on the Peter Gabriel record was a good one. The core of *So* was made with only three people: Peter, David Rhodes, and me. No drums or bass were used until much later in the project. It kind of sounds like a backward way of working: shouldn't you start with drums and bass first and then add everything else on top? Yes is the usual answer, except that Peter's songs were not fully written yet, and so my job was to chaperone the songwriting process. I chose to do that with as few people around as possible. David Rhodes lived nearby; we called ourselves the Three Stooges. Every day we turned up for work wearing yellow construction worker safety hats. I believe the song "Sledgehammer" came out of all that humor: *"Let's hit it with a sledgehammer!"* was part of our bravado and lingo. The entire foundation of the record was built on top of rhythm-box beats. Peter had done a lot of preparation with these beats, and as simple as some of them seemed to me at the time, I believe they were part of the success of our disciplined way of work.

David Rhodes and I played our guitars; Peter played his

keyboards and sang. The sparseness of this ensemble allowed the clarity of the songs to shine through. I could tell immediately if something felt right. There was not a lot of clutter to fool the ear. It's curious to hear the songs of *So* at that stage, before all the overdubs. The foundations had feel and soul like bread crumbs on a path—we could always find our way back. We could stray and venture off into experimentation, but the bread crumbs were always there to get us back to the source inspiration.

Because there were only three people in the room, it made it easy to change the course of how we were playing. Three people, or the triangle, is, in my opinion, the optimum for fast idea exchange. The bigger the ensemble, the bigger the ship—no fast turns, bad for spontaneity. There's something that happens when musicians stray from a planned or written arrangement, perhaps it's that place that jazz musicians go to. It's the feeling of freedom within a framework, connected to our human instinct to keep reinventing, changing, and modifying. Children certainly have it in them with playtime, that endless corridor of the imagination. I've seen that childlike euphoria come out of people in the recording studio, perhaps as a response to the pressure that studios seem to inherently exude. I love the aftermath of a take, where the musicians cut loose, jam out, have fun, take risks; those are often the best pieces.

When you're working with fixed time (as is the case when you're working to a beat box) you have the luxury of making use of the aftermaths by juggling them back into the main body of the song (with edits). The Peter Gabriel record benefited from this technique. "Sledgehammer," for example, busted into a long fun jam once the planned arrangement had run its course. Peter conjured up the most incredible spontaneous vocal ad lib, some of it nonlyrical or nonsensical, pure fun, jump-up-and-dance lines like "I've been feeding the rhythm"; "Show for me and I'll show for you"; "this is the new stuff I go dancing in." It was a shock to all of us. Were we not meant to be making a profound, mystical, West Country record? Peter, Rhodes, and I surrendered to this ride: an all-encompassing dance party, a kind of new craze, everybody included, family, friends, a bringing of the house, a rebirth, a celebration of life. The "Sledgehammer" video pretty much says it all. The unexpected jam-out became my favorite part of the song. I chopped the front part down so that we could fit in the crazy party ending. This has happened to me many times, where the unexpected becomes the thing I'm most excited about.

Peter Gabriel is made of good, he's made of dreams. His song "Don't Give Up" touched a lot of hearts because Peter addressed a real-life situation: a story of compassion at a time when work is not going well. We've all been at that bottleneck in life when sweet words of encouragement were necessary to cross a hurdle. Kate Bush stopped in to sing on "Don't Give Up" with Peter. I love the video for this song, Peter and Kate slowly spinning like two wedding cake figurines, a nice reminder that the simplest ideas are often the best. I'm still baffled by the curious bass line that Tony Levin played; he was just trying to mimic Peter's drum pattern. In fact, the song started out only as a drum pattern. The curious, slow evolution of "Don't Give Up" still mystifies me. The sentiment of this song is not very rock 'n' roll, but it might just outlive rock 'n' roll.

The West Country was magical in many ways, and I feel that my crossing into Peter's world had destiny attached to it. I lived in a tiny room upstairs from the studio. The source of heat was a small coal-burning fireplace. When I woke up in the night, I made journal entries, some work-related, like how to provide Peter with encouragement. Other entries were more dream-driven, perhaps emerging from a rapid-eye-movement state.

As usual i barely had things under control, not being familiar with this movie's music, and not necessarily being a fan.
The little that I have heard is well done. From it i feel tension, desperation, chill, respect and search. Also from it i do not feel Romance, satisfaction, contrast and happiness. These later qualities i believe i have an understanding of. The use of Human and earth tones will help this, such as treated pianos re: Harold Budd. Or the use of melodicas and combo organs re: Nino Rota Juliet of the Spirits.
Assuming that these more later qualities and moods will be required i feel confident that i can make a substantial contribution. If i can draw love from this man as well as expertise, my job is complete.

In preparation for this Peter Gabriel project, i must set up a monitor screen and music playback system, first at the house with a series of films such as, Days of Heaven, Koyaanisqatsi, and others, perhaps a reccomendation from Joe. Music on stand by: Juliet of the Spirits. Anthea's tape of Elgar. Harold Budd shimmering reeds, Jon Hassell's grand melody from Possible music. I must make a point of matching up scenes with music, perfectly. This match will give me strength to move on. For example why not improve Koyaanisqatsi (and send it to Coppola. or is it spelled Copola?) This set up can later be moved to Front with access to the 24. At this point i can experiment with compositions of mine.

pick up Melodica Hohner 27
" " movie: Days of Heaven
book some viewing time at Front
select one set of 4" tapes
" " of 2" masters

This two-page clip, from my Peter Gabriel work journal, is an example of a nighttime note to myself.

At this busy time, my books and diagrams were meticulously kept. Discipline is always a friend to business, and an organized book makes for organized work. Peter's control room didn't have very good ventilation, and I couldn't find a fan in England that I liked. So I shipped in one of my own from Canada—one of those big square beer drinkers' fans. That fan, wedged in the doorway of Peter's studio was my friend and my source of fresh West Country air, first for the making of *So*, and for this final stage of Robbie Robertson's solo record.

The humdrum of everyday life is a constant monster on my back. Nobody wants humdrum on a record; everybody wants magic. Robbie Robertson's storytelling ability was always magic to me. I loved listening to Robbie talk about his times in Arkansas with his buddy Levon Helm. I pushed Robbie to go into the labyrinth of the backwater swamp: dimly lit one-room shacks, sparsely spread out on the river's edge; one story led into another. The magic of the Delta, the birth of rock 'n' roll, the mixture of bluegrass, the slide guitar, the cotton-field songs, work songs mixed in with lust, the warble of Blind Willie Johnson, the darkness, the mystery, America finally admitting to its sexuality by embracing the blues, it was all there in "Somewhere Down the Crazy River." The little Suzuki Omnichord toy instrument that Eno had introduced me to had now been passed on to Robbie Robertson. The irregular chord sequences available on the Suzuki became the musical backbone to that song.

I'll be forever grateful to Peter Gabriel and U2 for helping me out with Robbie's record, as hosts and contributors. In their unspoken way, I believe they were proud that I was fighting for a Canadian comrade; pulling resources, available tools, and people together. Building a scene with my friends while trying to do good work. Scene building is very important.

When I was a kid in the early seventies, there was a cool scene back home in Hamilton. The YWCA had closed down, and somehow or other, a bunch of local bands had taken over the place. It was fantastic, two bands per floor, a strange blend of competition and brotherhood. It felt like there was some sort of cultural revolution at play, all kinds of people living there—musicians, runaways, drug dealers. This bizarre crossroads of energy became a mecca for hopefuls. It was a scene, and I love scenes. I was living with the legendary image of the Montreal poets' society that Leonard Cohen had been a part of, but that I had never experienced. There I was, living on the fourth floor of the YWCA, imagining that this was our time to build our own poets' society, in Hamilton of all places. Hamilton was a steelworker town that had been at one time a touring stop, sometime during the big-band era, but now we had to invent something else. The YWCA echoed rock 'n' roll, all day and all night; it had the smell of commitment. The scene did not last for long, but it sure gave me an appetite for more.

The ambient music chapter in Hamilton with Eno was a continuation of scene building (at least in my own head). Scenes are necessary because they are door openers. Why did Motown in Detroit suddenly have a cultural explosion? Why was Sun Studio in Memphis so prolific? Because they believed in building a scene. It was bigger than the actions of any one artist. The studio I would build later in New Orleans had a scene surrounding it. The rise of U2 in Dublin during the more industrial time of Temple Bar had a scene in it. Scenes are simply people collectively marching in a direction. Money may not buy it—collective thinking buys it.

I was not able to finish Robbie's record within the time allowed. I felt bad to leave him, but I had to return to U2 to stay on track with my calendar commitments. Robbie was kind; he said he could use the time for writing and sent me on my way with a blessing. We agreed to hook back up after *The Joshua Tree*.

Back in Ireland, everything was good. I went from living in Peter Gabriel's bell tower to an attic room in Adam Clayton's house. The first chapter of *The Joshua Tree* had gone well, and confidence was in the air after a successful initial start. The Edge has always managed to create a new guitar sound for each U2 album, and he had just received his infinite-sustain guitar, invented by my Canadian friend Michael Brook. It can be heard on "With or Without You," an infinite stratospheric sound never heard before. "With or Without You" was built with a technique similar to the Peter Gabriel one I spoke about: cut to a beat box with drums added last, but in this case Adam Clayton's bass part was put on early. Adam then had the luxury of concentrating on his work with a fully arranged song structure. I say luxury because Adam is often tossed around the studio in a constant wave of evolving chord progressions. Composing in the studio as U2 does often means that the bass part has to be redone to try and catch up to the new bit that somebody just wrote. But in the case of "With or Without You," the chords were carved in stone. Adam chose to play a new Japanese bass he had recently acquired; a nice short-scale instrument by Ibanez. Short-scale basses are like small grand pianos; the notes are the same as a larger instrument, but the strings are shorter. Some may regard a six-foot grand piano to be a lesser instrument than a nine-foot grand piano, but if you close your eyes there is a harmonic overtone to a shorter string that is musical and not to be surpassed by the longer string. The Gibson company made a series of short-scale basses that are absolute rockers, the EB series. I still use one myself. Play it soft, turn it up loud, it gives you a jukebox bottom. To apply physics as I understand it, the shorter string does not require as much tension as the longer string to reach the desired pitch, and so it flops around a little bit more, like a big soft rubber band. Adam delivered a fabulous performance on top of the Yamaha beat box. Beautifully played, it had infinity in itself, on top of the infinite-sustain guitar.

There was now a big beautiful hole in the center for Bono's lead vocal. His delivery had a quiet tension in it, like a lover expressing admiration and gratitude, while at the same time addressing the evolution of emotion; it was about change, really. We all change, which creates forks in the road. The path hasn't been wrong up to the fork, it just means there is new information to decipher and accommodate. It's about loving what you have, yet still wondering where it's going. The journey of love is represented in the arrangement of "With or Without You." Just when you think you've seen it all, the Edge comes in with the last kiss, delivering a memorable riff as the song fades out.

One production technique does not work for all songs. Sometimes it's best to accept a little piece of magic as a gift, and let that become the foundation for everything else. U2's "I Still Haven't Found What I'm Looking For" was built on top of one of these moments, created by the magic of Larry Mullen. A leftover drum track from a provisional title, "Under the Weather," had always haunted me, and I wanted this magic and original Larry Mullen effort to get on the U2 record somehow. These kinds of gems turn up and live in the orphanage of a record; by-products, essentially, or offshoots of what was meant to be the best-laid plan, they collect themselves into a sort of menu of good ideas. The unexpected bits and pieces are often the very interesting bits; I never throw them away. They may turn out to be the pieces that give a record its unique personality.

We were about to start the process of superimposition on "I Still Haven't Found What I'm Looking For." I regard this to be a relative to the technology of sampling. Sampling is done because people want to cop a good feel from an already existing record; instant gratification, really. In this case, we were not sampling from someone else's work; we were copping a feel from Larry Mullen Jr. The Edge, inspired by the Larry Mullen drum track, came up with an acoustic guitar part that had one foot rooted in gospel music. The chord changes were classic: 1–4–5, or C–F–G, like many classic songs ranging from "Blueberry Hill" to "Rock Around the Clock." Bono had a go at a vocal ad lib, and it all seemed to be pointing at rhythm and blues. My usual melodic whisperings in his ear mixed with his great lead-singer instinct to provide us with a futuristic church song. The Edge took a copy of the work home and came in the next day with a catchphrase: "But I still haven't found what I'm looking for." We had broken the back of it. Bono wrote his verses, Eno, the Edge, and I sang the group vocals, and it was all stacking up into something that felt right.

This song was a personal pet project, and I devoted a lot of time to the details. Adam and I must have tried twenty different bass lines to arrive at the ultimate hybrid that made the finish line. The Edge delivered a classic echo Stratocaster part. We must have had a go at the Stratocaster part a good dozen different times, always trying to improve the sound and delivery. Once the clock strikes midnight, the Edge is on some kind of natural speed; you better get ready, because you're gonna be up all night! Guys who have a lot of kids are used to the "up all night." The Edge also has an amazing capacity to remember all factual information; he might have been Einstein in another life. Nothing escapes the Edge. Definitely the scientist of the band.

The song was mixed at the Edge's house in a thrown-together control room, three of us hands on: the Edge, Pat McCarthy, and myself. When I listen to that song now, I can still feel the adrenaline pumping. We didn't use a computer mixing system. As musicians, we are capable of understanding the twists and turns of an arrangement. We love to know the position of our ingredients, we respond to an unexpected swell of the moment like a lover surprising you with a whisper, causing you to fall more deeply in love. A three-and-a-half minute song mixed with tender care by a dedicated team should add up to soul music. As I listen to "I Still Haven't Found What I'm Looking For" now, it sounds curious and eccentric; I could never repeat those sounds again, they belong to that moment in time.

I forget the reason, but sometime in the middle of *The Joshua Tree* we moved out of Adam's house down to the Edge's place, which hosted the building of "Where the Streets Have No Name." I missed the large rooms of Adam's house, but I believe the Edge's was better for mixing. One thing to note for those readers interested in the "gear": our monitors—a pair of Westlake Audio boxes with twin 12s—were always kept in a near-field position, so the room didn't get a chance to color our perspective. The speakers were always in our faces.

"Where the Streets Have No Name" was started by the Edge on his little home recorder. He had crafted a beautiful symphonic piece that shows up as the introduction, and sets the mood for the rest of the song. It was not easy to build onto because of odd bar lengths that made the process more scientific than the rhythm section would have liked, but once the groove got going, it was cool. I can well remember standing in front of this huge blackboard like a science teacher, pointing and conducting the band through the labyrinth of chord changes. The sound of speed is built into this song; I see telephone poles flying by every time I hear it.

There is a term that I like to use: liftoff. Liftoff is when all the ingredients gel and harmonic interplay works in your favor. Harmonic interplay is a result of a collision of ingredients. I suppose the best display of harmonic interplay would be a string quartet arrangement, or a four-part choral arrangement. In the case of the quartet or the choral arrangement, their design on paper would be a big part of their success. In the case of U2, the collisions are more abstract but essentially the same in the sense that there are usually four active ingredients.

Perhaps this is the right time to big up my friend Bono, as one of the great singers and improvisers. His ability to transform the direction of a piece of music is really something. Once he gets to that zone, it's like some other being has entered his body as he challenges the rest of us to rise to that same level of nonthinking, only performing. This is a wonderful magic place to get to, the room of splintered metal I call it, where you can only respond to what is thrown your way. Years of knowledge and life experience exorcized out of minds and bodies. The room of splintered metal and shattered glass is the birthplace of some of my U2 favorites: "Bullet the Blue Sky" was born there. "Elvis Presley in America" was born there. I suppose "Bad" could fall in the same category, and, for that matter, "Beautiful Day."

The time of *The Joshua Tree* was a time of great concentration. The houses had not been fully renovated, the children had not all been born, half of Dublin was still boarded up, and our workshop had a lot of alpha males in one room. We cared about our work deeply; I hope that level of care never goes away. One of the great pleasures for me is to hear the ultimate conclusion of my work at a U2 show. "Where the Streets Have No Name" found its ultimate glorious position when it provided the magic carpet ride for a stadium of sixty thousand people.

Back in Los Angeles, standing on the Santa Monica Pier outside the Shangri-La Hotel, I felt a wave of emotion relating to my work with Robbie Robertson. I didn't feel that L.A. was much of a friend to me. Robbie's record started out as a companion to a film idea called "American Roulette." As we progressed with our songs, the film association dissipated. I spent many hours at the pier contemplating life, wondering how and why we Canadians ended up in Los Angeles. Robbie and the Band made a great impression on me as a kid coming up in Canada. To a lot of us back home, Robbie was the living embodiment of adventure and excellence. There were times when I looked at the empty sky of Los Angeles and wondered if there was any rock 'n' roll left in it. I opened up my wallet and pulled out a tattered photograph of me and my girl. My hands wrapped in her raven hair, in a faded picture on the back stair.

We were narrow we were steady, trembling and ready to give it hell in this rocky world. You said, Do I look like I could be a strong mother? And raised the good side of a young daughter. In the hotel Shangri-La let me tell ya, I've been thinking of her in this rocky world. Jenny has religion, she sinks in her chair. She's made a decision to color her hair. While the black man cut the sugar cane, she watched the rain sheltered from this rocky world. Mon ami Romond, do you wonder maybe when you crawl into bed and you're half feeling dead, the mouth that you feed in the absence of greed. You've been working for something in this rocky world. Would you build me a building, a chapel out there at the top of the hill, in the still blue air? Near the weather vane, by the track and train.

Bury me in the rocky world. I'll tell you something I'll never forget, the sight of you in silhouette. Outside Sault St. Marie you really threw me when you pulled me down to your rocky bed in a crowded room I stood there empty, looking for salvation and glory. When a shot turned my head, I saw you instead walking into my rocky world.

I finished the Robby Robertson record on the sweet little API console in a backroom studio at A&M Records. The mixes were greasy, salty, punchy, and raw. I believe that the limitation of the equipment of that little mixing room pushed me to build clear and full-bodied blends. Sometimes a lack of options makes for better work. Robbie's record was remixed by Bob Clearmountain. It would be an interesting study to compare my greasy mixes against Clearmountain's mixes, now that much water has passed under the bridge.

7

LATE NIGHT AND HIGH NOON IN LOS ANGELES

One late night, Harry Dean Stanton did not want to go home. He was nervous about sleeping in his house because he had recently been robbed. Harry asked me if we could kill a few more hours until the sun came up. In my room at the Chateau Marmont hotel, he told me about his life—a wide range of experiences, from his love of traditional Mexican folk songs all the way to Buddhism. I asked Harry if he had any kids; he said he had one back east. He then told me that he had been with many great women and still had an eye for greatness. At that moment, an idea came into my head. A song idea about an angel who is the last visitor to a womanizer's lair.

I said to Harry:

You're traveling full speed and your heels are sliding down
  that muddy hollow
You've lost your grip and the distant call is feeble, it's
  nothing that you can follow
Desperation sends a shock to your brain now you must fight
Disintegrate the arms of your Brutus with her light

Harry play for your angel tonight. Your angel tonight
Let the water pass, let a stranger feel your power and esteem
Let him know your secrets, your passions none have ever
seen
While the beauties and the bloodless trample at your mat
Telling you do it again, but Harry watch your back
Harry play for your angel tonight. Your angel tonight
Your messages are branded on the face that holds a desperate
ugly scream
You've been running your charisma, down the walls of the
rusted dream machine
As you're lying there in your Cuban heels, there's not much
coming in
No transmissions, no interest, no offers on your skin
Harry play for your angel tonight, for your angel tonight
She always reaches deep and tells you she loves you from
her lip
Then you feel the silence escaping down to your fingertips
Harry play for your angel tonight, for your angel tonight
Harry play for your angel, come on let's hear you sing
We want to feel regret plummet down below the batting of
her wing
Remember what it was like to be driven to embrace
Before the years took their toll on that pretty face
Harry be with your angel tonight. She's coming tonight.
She's coming tonight.

Harry Dean Stanton left with the sunrise.

High noon, New Year's Day, L.A. I'm stirring my pot of soup. Two Mexican speed freaks appear in my kitchen out of nowhere, a foot from my face. I greet them with a "Happy New Year" and ask them "What's up?" and offer them each a beer. These guys are completely whacked out, sweating like pigs on crystal, crazed look in their eyes. They say they're lookin' for Tommy. I say Tommy's not here yet, would they like to play some pool? I give them a rant about the healing powers of my turkey soup. I criticize the grade of local crystal. I suggest to them that they get hip to Canadian crystal. Something about the humidity of the Canadian climate makes the crystal meth last longer. Better flavor. I threaten to kick both of their asses at pool.

My heart is racing, thinking that any second, one of them will pull a gun out of his knapsack. I think about Harry Dean Stanton; I should have been an actor. My friend Keisha walks in, she looks scarier than they do. I'm glad that that Russian jailhouse tattoo on her exposed stomach has found a practical use. She slips out, calls Gersh my neighbor. Gersh turns up with his weapon: a bottle of wine. The speed freaks are stupid, confused—maybe they think I'm crazier than them. I sink the last black ball. Gersh ushers them down the hill, out the gate. I take a breath, call the cops. The cops say that they have never heard of such a welcoming tactic, regarding speed-freak home invasion. I tell them: "I might be Canadian, but I grew up in a steel town. If you sense danger, you become one of them."

8

NEW YORK TO NEW ORLEANS

Any artist with a burning heart wants to live in New York City (or at least, any artist on the North American side of the pond). I was no exception.

New York City—the great crossroads for hopes and dreams. The underlying promise of NYC suggests that, by simply being there physically, you might just bump into other likeminded hopefuls, or other dreamers, or businesspeople looking for dreamers. If you make it to NYC, then you've "gotten on the bus."

I made two attempts to move to New York. The first was in 1983 when I took an apartment on MacDougal Street with a roommate by the name of Romano; the second was in 1988, at Tenth Street and University Place. The 1983 attempt was brief, as I ended up working in Ireland with U2 for the whole time, and in fact I didn't live in New York at all. Being a good Canadian, I kept paying my rent to Romano in spite of my never having turned up, beyond having bought some bedding and a few sticks of furniture.

The Macdougal apartment was just around the corner from where Eno had a place for a while. In fact, my fascination with

New York had arisen after my first visit to Eno's loft, where he lived for a brief patch. Eno had built a soundproof room for himself that he used for isolation from the din of the city. He had a nice rig of equipment, including a Revox reel to reel and a Stratocaster guitar. Eno placed the Stratocaster in my hands when I walked in the door, and in a matter of minutes, all kinds of sounds were pouring out of the speakers.

Eno had obviously been preparing his sounds prior to my arrival. My walking in completed the two vital ingredients: a fresh naïve musician and a fantastically prepared sonic room of delights. We were like two kids in a sandbox, his preparations mixed with my guitar melodies. This is the formula Eno and I operate by—always bring something to the table.

There was a tiny window that Eno kept a video camera in, shooting the rooftop landscape of SoHo. He never moved the camera, the only change was the light of the city, and whatever color manipulations he made on the few controls on board the camera. Occasionally birds cut across the frame for some action, otherwise it was a beautiful still frame with changing colors, like the changing of the seasons.

This visual work was related to what Eno had been working on in our sound recordings back in Canada: gentle shifts in mood, but not hard cuts. I liked this contradiction: serenity against the manic pace of NYC. Eno didn't keep his place for long; perhaps New York had said what it needed to say. SoHo had had its artistic heyday. Yes, the artists had moved in and elevated a dilapidated warehouse neighborhood to a happening cultural crossroads. By 1981, the high rents of SoHo were attracting designer ware and pushing out the up-and-comers. Manhattan was not about to let up. The mutual-fund brigade was coming in to take command. Commerce leads the way, even if it means pushing the artists to the outer limits. Brooklyn? When I squinted, I could feel the energy of the Ramones, Nico and Lou Reed, Andy Warhol, and the rise of punk. Eno didn't want to be in New York anymore. Sometimes it's best to leave the party early.

Even though my first New York move did not pan out, it was certainly the start of a long journey of drifting through different cultures, either from work invitations or driven by thirst for information. When I hear about the lives of sailors or ranch hands, who move according to work availability, I feel that I have traveled in a similar way. Perhaps the melancholy of my music comes from this drift. Questioning, searching, learning—all of this is a running away of sorts, but I'd rather be running than be caught in the bear trap of suburban life. A lot of my time has been spent in hotels, and there is a wisdom to that. A front desk to deal with packages, acquisition kept at bay, a good setting for concentration, and somebody else to do the gardening.

I kept working in Europe for a while. Nose to the grindstone, my skills were high and my concentration was even better. By the time I left, the records I had worked on there had become massive hits. Peter Gabriel's *So* album had ubiquitously taken the world, and U2's *The Joshua Tree* had been received as a force of its time. A second try at New York City put me at Tenth and University—an already furnished apartment in a corner brick building, with a diner on the ground floor. The natural light was bad, but the place was cute. The woman I was renting from had four ropes tucked under the bed, each tied to a bedpost. I never put them to use, but I bet she had.

Perhaps the New York I was looking for had already passed by in time. The Washington Square Park that I had read about was now a tourist hangout. The East Village was on the rise, but the university area and the West Village did not have a lot of bohemia left in them. The New York that once welcomed the artist with a small pocketbook was evolving into a place for only the rich.

I was lonely in New York, but I didn't mind. After all, I didn't know anyone there. There I was, a musician with no instruments, and so off to Forty-eighth Street to pick out some gear. It was all there: Manny's Music (where Jimi Hendrix had acquired his Stratocasters) and We Buy Guitars (run by the Friedman family, from whom I later bought many fine pieces). The Forty-eighth Street shopping trip provided me with all I needed to write songs for my first record. This was my setup: a used Les Paul Junior with gold Grover keys, and a used Jazzmaster also with gold Grovers; a 16-channel Hill mixer and a twelve-track Akai analog recorder, monitoring line-in through a blaster, and a Korg delay unit to plug my guitar into, which the Edge had introduced me to, and which I still use today. The setup was fantastic, no noises from cooling fans because the equipment didn't have any. I still look for equipment that has no cooling fans to this day.

My head was buried in that blaster for a good few months, and I became master of the Korg echo box. My custom-made sounds became an extension of my fingers, heart, and soul. Those sounds became part of who I was, and I was proud to have risen above the level of generic store-bought presets.

This seems like a good time to talk about the importance of choosing one's tools. Confidence building is really at the heart of this matter, and I strongly believe that making choices with regard to tools is the beginning of finding one's voice. It's about believing that a song lives in a guitar, by just looking at it up on a wall. You can think of it as a sort of crystal ball: the capacity to see the future of a song. I have always had a high regard for tools, and I care for them the best I can. When they break or get dusty, I know my life needs readjustment.

I love New York City as I love all large cities—waves of hopes and dreams, so many hearts pushing and pulling. It's all fascinating, as I believe that we are designed to do best in villagelike settings, whose smaller populations lead to greater compassion and care for others. And yet we build these incredible massive urban centers where the weak have little chance.

My music started taking shape. All that loneliness funneled down to my music. I had found my own voice at the age of thirty-five. I picked up a magazine that had a feature on New Orleans—beautiful black-and-white photographs of street performers, with old French and Spanish architecture surrounding them. "That's where I should finish my songs," I decided, and so I packed up my belongings and took the train to New Orleans.

Echoes of Fats Domino, the Meters, Little Richard, and Louis Armstrong rang in my head as I rode the train through the backside of towns from New York to Louisiana. The poverty struck me sharply and I could see evidence of a shifting economy and culture. The steel industry had subsided considerably back home in Hamilton, and I could see the same sort of remission in the northern American towns. I guess it was all part of the begining of fewer goods being manufactured in North America. Cheap foreign labor was starting to have a visible effect.

The farther south I went, the more old-fashioned the disintegration looked. The very poor small towns through Mississippi were likely the same as they had been for a long time. The decline of the steel industry in the north did not apply here. These were full on, very poor, old black neighborhoods. I was pretty much fearless back then, and my naïve way of looking at situations was very much part of my strength. Naïveté is an interesting trait; it can help one dive into a situation, even at the risk of being wrong. It's a curious part of one's instinct; it might be a survival intelligence, perhaps it's related to "love is blind." How many times have I found myself working three times harder than I initially anticipated? The answer is every time.

I arrived in New Orleans. It was dilapidated and beautiful.

Lots of boarded-up buildings in the areas of commerce, little wooden shotgun houses, multicolored like a display in a candy store. My little apartment was a guesthouse on Saint Ann Street in the French Quarter. The place was run by a couple who had left England for warmer weather and a more exotic life. I liked the apartment, made up of three rooms and a bathroom. The ceilings were high, which is good for sound.

Brian Patti, my old friend from Canada, had kindly agreed to drive some of my equipment from Canada down to New Orleans. The Patti had beaten me there, and so he greeted me at the train station with a smiling face. The Patti said he was not sure about this place, something felt wrong, and his instinct caused him to advise me against New Orleans. Part of me wishes I had listened.

The next few months were prolific times, as I fell into the depths of guitar playing and songwriting. I had no phone, so I would walk to a nearby hotel to use the pay phone when I needed it. In the age of the cell phone, such a limitation might be good for these contemporary times: more action, less talk.

My apartment was right by Rampart Street near Congo Square. The square had been a place of congregation, stretching back to slavery days, a meeting place where the black folks of that time were permitted to play drums and sing songs, what part of them they could remember from back in Africa.

Then there is the legend of the Mardi Gras Indians to bring into the equation. Displaced Native Americans had also congregated at Congo Square. Legend has it that runaway slaves were guided by the Native Americans to a new village life, hidden in the backwaters of the Louisiana swamps. The adaptation of the fancy native dress by the blacks was the birth of the Mardi Gras Indians tradition, which exists to this day.

Every neighborhood has a tribe. The Pretty White Eagles is one, another is called the Ninth Ward Hunters, there are the Wild Magnolias, and most significant to myself, the Wild Tchoupitoulas. Significant to me, because the Wild Tchoupitoulas include the presence and talent of the great Neville family. The Neville Brothers came up through the ranks of their tribe. Their uncle Jolly had taught them the old songs, songs designed to build testosterone and confidence, like the bagpipe does for the Scotsman; the Mardi Gras Indian chants were built to boost unity and identity within a neighborhood gang. Working with the Neville Brothers allowed me to enter this wonderful world.

They say that the funk comes from the tuba. The high humidity content in the air of New Orleans provides a tuba player with a better seal at every gasket, at every valve, and in the way the Sonar signal of a whale reaches a long distance with the water as its transmitter, the New Orleans thick moist air is a loyal, relentless conductor of tone.

The parade drumming pounds, the appetite for celebration never subsides. The unveiling of the costumes on Mardi Gras is still a source of great pride to the Indians and their communities. In New Orleans, neighborhood is the teacher of music and tradition. Back in Quebec when I was a kid, I felt the strength of neighborhood. There was not a lot of money to go around, so the folks were self-entertaining; visiting one another's houses and bringing the kids along was normal. The adults would go crazy playing cards all night, while the kids were piled up in a bed in a room. As I mentioned earlier, my grandfather and my dad were *violoneux*. Busting out the violins was all part of the celebration. It didn't take much for the night to break into song, and there was some kind of genius to the music rising up at the pinnacle of the night. Music was never background; if it existed, it existed in the foreground, and when the violins went back in their cases, it was time for more laughter and more storytelling. That rule is still with me now. I hate music to be background. If you want music, make music; if you want food, make food—not the two at once.

New Orleans was good to me; I felt I had come to the right place. I could work on my own music there and learn plenty about the source of rock 'n' roll. Jim Phelan, my manager at the time, put two and two together. The Neville Brothers live in New Orleans; let's get Lanois producing a Neville Brothers record. So there we were, the Neville Brothers and me, in my new and bigger apartment. Still in the Quarter, but now an upstairs place with lots of steps—not a friend to Art Neville's Hammond B-3 organ. The demos went well; Aaron Neville wanted to record a version of Bob Dylan's "Ballad of Hollis Brown," which turned out great. Live off the floor, vocal and all, I mixed the song on my Hill mixer to a Sony cassette deck. I never bettered the mix, so I used the cassette as the master. Much confidence came out of the demo sessions, and so the Nevilles and I decided to jump into the full swing of a record.

At this point I had just employed this kid, Mark Howard from Canada, to be my assistant. Howard had had a lot of road experience, so he was very resourceful in regard to setups. I challenged him to find us a location for the record, and he did find one. An apartment building, of all places, was about to become the home for the Neville Brothers' *Yellow Moon* album—a nice old six-story building, complete with one of those cool old accordion-gate elevators. I lived on the top floor, the studio lived on the second floor, Howard and Malcolm Burn, whom I had employed to help me with engineering, lived on some other floors. It was pretty much a mattresses-on-the-floor scenario. Charles Neville lived in the basement. This was on Saint Charles, one of the main boulevards in New Orleans.

In those days, I offered record companies a package deal. The offer was simple: pay me one hundred and fifty thousand dollars, and I'll deliver you a great record, no questions asked. Rather than piss away the money on someone else's studio, I simply assembled gear and personnel and guaranteed my label a full heart-and-soul operation and result. For the Nevilles, I brought in a PA console, made by a great British company called Amek. Amek had served me well in Ireland, 36 channels, more than I needed to do good work, great equalizers, and a good punch to the summing amplifiers. I held on to this beast for years, and I hated to let it go, but the crackling pots finally got to me. I eventually sold it to Pearl Jam (if memory serves me right).

Back to the Nevilles. My gear was limited—just a few effects boxes and a few external Neve mic preamps. Lots of dynamic mics, often hitting the onboard Amek mic preamps, because I thought they had a sound. Good for drum miking and guitar amp miking, etc. The Neves were kept for the singing. My recorder was a two-inch Studer A80 wide body. I still have it, 24 channels of Dolby running at 15 i.p.s.; great sound. The computer age would render this masterpiece of technology practically worthless. Evolution of economics is powerful; a cheaper way of doing things will usually win out. I was sad to see Technicolor disappear, and I am sad to see the A80 disappear.

The Neville Brothers' record was going well, the vibe was thick and significant. Bob Dylan happened to be touring in Louisiana, and my agent Bono had gotten me on the phone to arrange a rendezvous for Dylan and myself. Bono has a good instinct about him, and I believe he thought that this matchmaking was perfectly timed. Dylan, of course, had come up through the amazing cultural revolution of New York City. He was used to renegade behavior, having broken a few rules along the way himself.

Dylan walked into my studio and I knew he had an appetite for dedication. He had a vibe on him like a boxer who had fallen out of the limelight, looking to come back in to regain his throne. There was nothing to be discussed about the past. I knew he was a futurist, even if he was fighting for a position in the present. Dylan was touring nonstop, and I can remember a few heads saying to me that it was too much. In retrospect, Dylan was right to stay on the road. No time to get fat, firmly devoted to his first love. A performer must have his audience.

I had created a vibe on Saint Charles, and Bob felt it when he walked in. The studio was built for speed; no shred of performance could escape me. My crew was eating and breathing the Neville Brothers. No distractions, no phone calls regarding other work, no disturbances, one thing at a time, celebrate the moment—just like the violin players of Quebec.

The renegade setup promoted commitment and, as usual, an appetite for innovation was at the forefront. Respect for tradition was unspoken, but clearly the spine of our work. You don't make a Neville Brothers record without having done your homework. The forefathers and mothers were ghosts and guardian to all—cotton-field singers, Lee Dorsey, the Meters, Uncle Jolly, Professor Longhair, Dr. John, to name a few of the angels looking down upon us. The city that had spawned jazz had kindly laid out a welcome mat to me, the traveling Canadian. If I could align myself for a minute with Alan Lomax (one of the great field collectors of folk music, who recorded hundreds of artists across the states), my forays into this Neville Brothers' neighborhood never crossed the line of respect.

Bob Dylan listened to a few songs of the Nevilles' record, including a version of his own "God on Our Side" sung by Aaron Neville. Aaron's performance was riveting, and at the end of the playback, Bob looked at me and said, "That sounds like a record." After some philosophical exchange, we agreed to hook up in the spring and make his next album. Bob is no fool; he knew that something was going on here. The entire package appealed to him. All he needed to do was turn up on the doorstep, and Lanois would have everything ready to go. Perhaps Bono had been right about this matchmaking. Synchronicity was at play, and a Dylan-Lanois dark-night record was on the horizon.

The Nevilles lived on Valence Street around the corner, except for Charles, of course, who was living in the basement of the studio complex. It made it easy for everybody to go home and chill if need be, while I prepared the studio for the next bit of work. New Orleans was special to me, and I gave it all I had. My research and study in anticipation of making the Nevilles' record had taken me to different people's houses, seeking out inspiration for song material. Art had dug up an old pile of cassettes of the Meters rehearsing back in the day. They were barely decipherable to a Canadian, but the rehearsal banter between the drummer, Zigaboo, and the rest of the band was impressive. I understood where the funk came from—from the hearts of young men carrying the torch of the groove. It was something to be taken, in my opinion, as seriously as anyone might take Stravinsky, Mozart, or Beethoven.

I felt blessed as my education broadened—to be exposed to this kind of phrasing felt like knives stabbing into me. To be in a room with Art, Aaron, Cyril, and Charles, that was something else. Aaron had a stack of lyrics, some that he had written in jail. In fact, the title song, "Yellow Moon," had come from the big house; Aaron with a tattoo of a dagger on his face, singing to the moon and wondering if his girl is missing him. I wish that song had become a hit; I think it's some of my best work. Every note drips with excellence. So much has to be aligned for music to reach the masses. I can only do what I can do, and then I wait to see if others can carry the work to its next position. That's life.

Any instinct that I might have as a commercial animal is not even there at the beginning of a record. Perhaps it's a part of the process for making records that have soul. I let everything unfold naturally, all ideas considered, even song choices. Never say no. As time travels, some song or some part of the record will raise its hand as the commercial member of the family. That's when the doors open. Product managers are welcome, radio programmers, publicists, and support systems. Come one, come all to the table. Once the identity of an album has been found and the likely hits earmarked, I like having businesspeople around; they will carry the torch while I sleep.

Eno agreed to help me with the Neville recordings. This was before the commercial part of the recording, when we were still children chanting in the sandbox. I loved having Eno around with his nonstop stream of sonics. The Nevilles were very curious about him. At an impressed moment, Art Neville leaned over to me, pointed at Eno, and whispered in my ear: "Where did you find this cat?" Art was so impressed with Eno's sonics that he paid him the greatest compliment, "That's some cold-blooded shit," and then the ultimate compliment: "That's some other kind of shit." Art knew what he was talking about. Check out his hit from the fifties called "Mardi-Gras Mambo"—definite soul, with a kick-ass sax solo, tone big as a house.

Eno was living next door. I had gotten him a nice big suite at the old Columns Hotel. The vibe of the place was such that it could have been a hundred and fifty years ago. I was happy to have my friend with me. Eno's presence on the Nevilles' record is a nice reminder about the surprises of life, and that spontaneous invitations should always be put into motion at the moment of mischievous conception.

The Nevilles' record was finished with dignity. All input from all the brothers had been accommodated: Cyril's political stance properly echoed in the recording of "Sister Rosa"; Aaron had sung "God on Our Side"; Charles's saxophone instrumental won us a Grammy Award; and Art is there in spite of much personal hardship, with the loss of his woman's life. I never knew all the details. There were a few times when I had to go to his house to cheer him up and convince him to come to work. I love Art, he's one of the world's greats. The Canadian school system might teach you breathing technique, but standing next to Art Neville will teach you how to phrase from soul places unknown.

My own music was streaming through cracks of available time. My little baby Fender Mustang guitar had provided me with a lonely instrumental that I nurtured, edited, and built into a sonic sculpture. In fact, I named this piece of music "White Mustang," ultimately completed with a full Eno backdrop atmosphere. At the early stages of building "White Mustang," I heard the most beautiful muted trumpet sound wafting through the window of my New Orleans apartment. I stuck my head out and there he was—a street performer set up on the cobblestones, top hat on the ground, playing beautifully. I could not believe he was playing in the same key as my song. I ran down and introduced myself. He said his name was James May. James agreed to play on my song for a set fee. I helped him pack his few things, and we spent the next hour recording trumpet on "White Mustang." His soul was intact, and I am thankful to James May for his gift. He and I have done a few other things since; in fact, I saw him in New Orleans somewhat recently and he asked me if I could embellish his original payment with a few extra bucks, given that "White Mustang" had turned up on an episode of *The Sopranos*; of course I was happy to oblige. Katrina left a lot of musicians hollow, but James was the same as he had always been. The cascading melody of James May still rings in my head.

My next move was over to Soniat Street, to a classic wooden house with a brick drive and enough privacy to accommodate

Mr. Dylan for the making of his *Oh Mercy* album. The house also had a swimming pool, and Jane Birkin was living up the street. I befriended two little boys, twins, about eight years old, and they loved hanging around. I believe they were living with their grandparents, single mom working, daddy-o missing—classic story. The kids liked to draw, and if the drawings were good enough, I paid them a few bucks and stuck them on my refrigerator. I became their source of income. I had an old '65 Cadillac in those days, and car washing added to the twins' income. I quickly put a stop to all that when I caught them washing my Caddy with S.O.S pads. Saturday was swimming day. What started out as the two boys swimming evolved into every neighborhood kid dive-bombing into my pool. It got way out of control, and so I asked my friend Christine to act as lifeguard. In retrospect, the swimming thing was a huge liability, but I am kind and Canadian, and we Canadians don't sue people, so I let them swim, and a good time was had by all.

Dylan turned up as planned with a set of songs. A few of them I had already heard on the piano back at his place. One of my favorites, called "Most of the Time," was still haunting me. I had already designed the bass line in my head, and in fact that's the line I played, and the one that made the finish line. The *Oh Mercy* studio was essentially a kitchen. Bob and I sat like two guys on a porch. He played on my nice 1952 butterscotch Telecaster that I plugged into an early sixties Fender Concert amp tucked around the corner, five feet from Bob, with moving blankets around the mic to avoid vocal spill. When Bob moved on to the acoustic guitar, he played my Gibson Country Western model (circa late fifties). I used a Lawrence clip-on pickup, and ran the acoustic through the same Fender Concert; so Bob's guitar sound was always coming out of the same amp, electric or acoustic. As for myself, I mostly played my steel-bodied Dobro from the twenties, its neck as thick as an oar, through a Fender blackface Twin head that was powering a Champ speaker, pretty low volume. That was the rig; we never changed it. My red Peavey bass from Mississippi was plugged in DI, and at the end of the night if we had a take, I would overdub the bass part. Malcolm Burn, who was engineering, had a couple of keyboards at the console, and he was always welcome to play along. I had my Vox AC30 amplifier in a cubbyhole for louder parts, as can be heard on "Most of the Time"—distant distorted guitars, like a chamber orchestra of Les Paul Juniors. The Vox and Les Paul rig, turned all the way up to 10. Bob sang into one of my Sony C-37As, acquired in Canada when they were refurbishing the sound system at Massey Hall. Nobody knew much about Sony tube mics back then, and I believe I singlehandedly drove up the price of these Sonys by bragging about them in interviews. I still have my original, the same mic I would later use on Bob's voice for *Time Out of Mind*.

Bob was private and punctual, never wasted any time, still one of the most focused people I've ever worked with. I had a little coffee machine that he would wander up to, as he stood touching up his lyrics. A drum kit was set up to my right, Bob sat to my left, and if we needed a drummer, I'd call in Willie Green, drummer for the Nevilles and one of New Orleans's funkiest. Willie lived in the next neighborhood. How cool is that?—"Mean Willie Green," one fast phone call away. I thanked the gods for having dropped me down into this rich musical environment.

> Outside the boundary line where numbers don't add up
> Beyond segregation, below down on your luck
> Temptation—love way out of balance,
> In a wooden shack, over on Valence
> Pictures of Jesus, memorabilia,
> Cold air blowing on Ophelia

Rats swaggin' on wires, '65 Cadillac,
Gonna buy up a lot of things if Daddy ever come back
Scraping of the wagon wheel
Orange steel
Abandoned couches on the medium
Men fighting off the tedium
Outside the boundary line where nobody adds up.
The numbers below down on your luck.

We experimented with a few guest musicians, including Rockin' Dopsie's band, to back us up. Dopsie was a great zydeco artist, one of the last remaining old-school rock 'n' rollers of America. I say "was" because he passed away in 1993. His band sounded fantastic, great rhythm section and a great sax player named Johnny Hart. I loved Johnny's playing—full-bodied, fat sexy sound, lots of air and feeling. Clearly he had not been touched by the unfortunate evolution of the saxophone tone, that terrible squeaky sound that contemporary sax players have generally adopted. *Uptown memories—me standing looking in the window of an old storefront, Dopsie's drummer sitting in the window, the place goin' crazy—Saturday night at the Maple Leaf Lounge.*

Dopsie's band offered a strange Lafayette dance-hall feeling to the Dylan record, as heard on the track called "Shooting Star." The Dopsie sessions were cut short when we realized that Dopsie could play in only two keys, D or G. The button accordion is a great but limited instrument. I still have a few rolls of two-inch tape of Dopsie's band demonstrating the various Lafayette grooves that could have been on Bob's record.

"Ring Them Bells" is one of my favorites from the *Oh Mercy* album, a fantastic live vocal and piano performance from the man himself. There's something special about the cohesion of a one-point source, when the piano and the vocal are done simultaneously. Bob performed "Ring Them Bells" at my rented Steinway B, which I later purchased and recently sold to John Cusack. John loves "Ring Them Bells," and so now he has my piano at his place in Chicago.

The sessions started later and later every day, and we were soon working only at night. Bob trusted the night as the record became more dark and mysterious. It got to a point where Bob was suspicious of any work done in the daytime; only nighttime work was allowed. I've heard it said that different tempos and rhythms are pleasing to our bodies relative to the time of day. Nighttime pushes the tempos slower, and tonalities are likely to be deeper and more profound after dark. The song "Man in a Long Black Coat" was born in and inspired by the nights of New Orleans, a view of a life without adventure that sees a chance for a new beginning, a sort of run-away-and-join-the-circus story. Bob was inspired, and I was proud of our progress, though I know that part of him was pining for more of a full-band setup, which had served him well in the past. There were moments of insecurity regarding our back-porch-kitchen-with-two-chairs approach, but we had a great vocal sound, and I felt that our nucleus was intact.

A certain kind of communication exists at the small table, two people keeps it tight, a safeguard against boardroom opinion. Small tables are not boardroom tables. Eno once said to me, "I'll agree with whatever you say if you agree with whatever I say." There's nothing worse than an outside opinion if it contradicts the direction of the record I'm interested in. A table for two—one pair of eyes stares into the other on a handshake, no other opinions are considered. The world loves a record that is specific in its stance. I will gladly embrace dictatorship if it creates a better chance for potent directed work. The setting for *Oh*

Mercy promoted a "staring eyes" feeling—one pair of eyes staring into another, or out into the darkness of New Orleans. The chance encounter of Dylan and I had established a secret and mysterious tone; like a train passing through a station without making a stop. We were on our own, we could do whatever we wanted. Sometimes freedom is frightening. *Oh Mercy* has been a constant source of compliments, from people who listen to records. A record may be bought, but will a record be played? *Oh Mercy* lives on in the playlists of those who listen.

Mark Howard and I had acquired some cool old Harley-Davidsons that Dylan liked, and so Mark found Bob a real beauty. He rode that bike around New Orleans, and I can imagine the freedom he felt, not only from the bike experience but a freedom away from the usual duties at more familiar turf. The record took shape, material took a direction, and a few songs fell by the wayside. One of my personal faves, called "Series of Dreams," later turned up on a bootleg, but was not on the official record. "Series of Dreams" had frailty in it and testimony, and as I hear it now, Bob might have been right to leave it off *Oh Mercy.* Maybe it should have existed on *Time Out of Mind.* The shame about being expert and knowledgeable is that when you are in the depths of your work, you have the least amount of objectivity. If a button could be pushed to fully cleanse the palate and beam you back into the situation with a full sense of awareness, that's the button I'd pay any amount of money for. Leaving off "Series of Dreams" might have been the right decision, but it might have been the wrong one.

I've always been a fan of Dylan's paintings and drawings. I love his hockey player painting, used by the Band on their LP cover for *Music from Big Pink.* I also love Dylan's painting for his own album *Self Portrait.* Before we parted, I asked Bob if he could do a charcoal drawing of me, and he did. But he did not sign it. Later that night, in a heavy rain, the doorbell rang; it was Bob, soaking wet at the gate. He had come back to sign the little drawing. I was touched. We spoke a bit about dreams, and I felt that I had not only made a good record for Bob, but that I had opened a door for him to look through with a view of the future. Ten years later we would meet again.

My first record, *Acadie*, was finished in the Soniat house with the ghost of Bob Dylan at the coffee machine. The setup stayed the same, and I regard my record as stage three of the New Orleans trilogy: *Yellow Moon* first, *Oh Mercy* second, and then my *Acadie*. Distance from my home turf clarified stories from the past. A lot of confidence had come my way regarding my sonics, largely through the trenches I had been fighting in with U2, Peter Gabriel, and for that matter, Eno, but I believe my time with Bob inspired me to look at my own life stories. Enough time had passed, and my geographical distance brought me clarity, and my songs poured out. My mother, packin' up four kids and driving five hundred miles away from my dad, of course showed bravery, but I decided to look at the situation through the eyes of my father. A man who hits the bottle might lose his kids, but that doesn't mean that he has lost his love for them.

All the images in my head were clearly Canadian. The Grand River cutting through the Six Nations reserve, the native eyes that I had stared into, eyes with alcohol in them, were the eyes of inspiration for my song "Still Water," a song that explains departure, but a song that is also there for the return. Tobacco picking in Ontario is a dirty-dog job, historically performed by young French Canadian men workin' for the Anglo farmers. My song "Oh Marie" describes the labor and the backbreaking disintegration of morale. The best money-saving intentions might all go out the window, come the weekend blowout at the tavern in town. *"Ma blonde elle attend après moi,"* means "My girlfriend, she waits for me," but the man who returns from the tobacco farm with his money already spent might not be able to keep his girl.

Images of the Great Lakes, snowbanks crystallizing at a mild weather moment, freezing back down to thirty below zero, branches of trees ready to give up the ghost under the strain of a three-inch-thick coat of ice, freight train rides, the great blue heron landing on the Speed River, the sequoia pines threatened by logging. The lonely whistle of the prairie wind, and me drifting like a gambler.

All images intact, relating to true experiences in Canada. That is my *Acadie.*

9

BEAUTIFUL DAY

By-products are never underestimated in my line of work. They might suddenly become the unexpected jolt that unlocks the door to the fabulous unknown . . . to a beautiful day.

It all began when Bono brought a chord sequence to the table that the Edge adapted, and that became the backbone to a song. Many days were spent knocking the sequence around, mostly in the band room, where it is noisy and bombastic. Like working in the open hearth of a steel mill, the heat is such that you can't remove your fireproof suit. Instructions are given by hand signal, and pouring the burning ingots requires muscle from all.

After much labor, "Beautiful Day" was not beautiful yet. It had a good foundation rooted in the tradition of Bo Diddley, or Iggy Pop's "Lust for Life," but the sound of it was a bit stuck in the barroom, and as usual our expectations were high. We wanted to feel the future and not just the past.

Eno and I historically have turned up at the U2 studio in the early morning before the band's arrival. Not too many words get said, he and I plug in and get our sounds going. Eno had been frustrated by the lack of progress with the engine room versions, and so he dialed up a beat-box rhythm and played a piano and string part over top as I laid on a Telecaster part that related harmonically to the Edge's chord sequence. The Telecaster part played the third above the Edge's root, providing a choral quality, like harmony singing. The beat box gave the song a feeling of speed and travel. I should take this moment to emphasize that Eno is one of the great interpreters. His ability to present a new angle on an already existing theme remains unsurpassed. When the band came in, there was a good mood in the air; everybody could feel the fresh angle.

Larry was able to play a triplet feel against the beat box, and Adam could now hold the beast down with his Clayton–Bo Diddley riff. It was all stacking up, and as usual when the vibe gets good, the ideas start flowing. The Edge's sound got greasier by the bar, and at the end of the twenty-minute version, it was sounding like shattered, splintered metal coming at you like a meteor storm. It was a high-life euro-rock euphoric sensation, and just like "Sledgehammer," the outro lifted off, and out of nowhere, Bono shouted: "And it's a beautiful day/Beautiful day/Don't let it get away."

After the lunch break, Eno and I rushed back to our stations and transferred Bono's "beautiful day" shout to earlier places in the jam, and the song started taking shape. The outro soon became our chorus, and the luxury of fixed time allowed us to move the "beautiful day" outro section to be chopped in as the chorus for the rest of the song.

The Edge and I picked up mics as Bono encouraged us to sing background vocals to the now new choruses. I sang a low doo-wop melody—a sort of distant relative to "The Lion Sleeps Tonight" as the Edge sang a high fifth above me at the top of his range. We doubled them up, and then Eno processed our singing and turned us into a choir.

Bono then built the bridge. He had had an idea about looking at Earth the way the astronauts could see it from outer space, a view of human existence without boundaries, from the aboriginal bonfires of Australia to the shooting stars over the tundra. Bono took the track home and wrote his verses. I'm leaving a lot out regarding mixes and all, but that was pretty much the building process. It was a lot of fun. The running of a relay race has selflessness built into it. You carry the stick for five hundred yards, to then hand it to your mate for their five hundred yards. You cannot win the race on your own. The best days in the studio with a team are days of relay.

10

THE BELLS OF OAXACA

I didn't know whether to barrel through the roadblock—or stop. There were ten people holding a rope across the little Mexican road. I thought for sure I would kill them if I drove through, so I stopped. They were roadside beggars, asking for a donation for having fixed up the road. You hear stories about Mexico and how you can easily get robbed in this fashion. I gave them some money, tried my best to speak Spanish; they tried their best to speak English.

A chance encounter with Sally Grossman had fueled my enthusiasm for making this trip to Oaxaca. Sally's husband, Albert, managed Bob Dylan back in the day; he was a giant of a man, well known in New York City for his wisdom and guidance at the rise of rock 'n' roll, not only for Bob Dylan, but for other artists like Ian and Sylvia and the Lovin' Spoonful. I met Albert briefly before he passed. He had a fatherly aura about him, and part of me wishes that he had been around for my initial *Oh Mercy* work with Bob Dylan, but he was already gone. Sally had kindly invited me to make use of her house, in a small village in the hills outside Oaxaca. If memory serves me right, this was around

1990. I had finished an avalanche of work, including U2's *The Joshua Tree*, Peter Gabriel's *So,* Bob Dylan's *Oh Mercy*, Robbie Robertson's solo album, the Neville Brothers' *Yellow Moon*, and my own *Acadie*. I felt good, but my brain was a muddle from work. I wanted my Mexican sabbatical to rest my brain, but also to broaden my education.

There's something about Mexican music that I've always loved. It sounds great on the jukebox. It's the bass, really. Deep bass had brought me south to New Orleans, and my hunger for bass was about to take me south again, this time south of the Mexican border. I'm still trying to figure out Mexican bass lines. They are deep in tone and complex in phrasing, distantly related to Argentinean dance music or Cuban salsa. Mexican music must have had a similar historical evolution to the zydeco music of Louisiana: both have bass lines designed with dance and celebration in mind. If you want to understand a form, go to the source, and so . . . off to Mexico.

My first stop between Mexico City and Oaxaca was Puebla, a Spanish-style town, with evidence of wealth in its architecture. The city center was sweet, little shops feeding life, the food store, the clothes store, the toy store, and the coffin store. Where I grew up, I never saw a coffin store. Coffins were kept hidden, until somebody died. In Mexican culture, everyday life sits closer to death, the way that in French culture, everyday life sits closer to sex.

The single-lane mountain road from Puebla to Oaxaca was blocked for a good eighty miles by a traveling circus caravan going ten miles per hour. With dangerous cliff drop-offs, there was no passing the caravan. In the car I was listening to Miles Davis's *Kind of Blue*: its city sound blended curiously with the passing mountain ranges. I finally made it to Sally's bed, in a tiny mountain village up above Oaxaca, but the rain kept me awake, pitter-patter all night. I went outside in the pitch blackness, but there was no rain. What I was hearing was the sound of termites eating the roof of the house. Two bats lived in there with me, and a donkey guarded the back gate.

Sally's house had no hot water, and so I bathed in midday sun. For someone who had largely been an urbanite, the silence of the mountain village was a new experience. The silence was so deep, it gave the word *lonely* a whole new meaning. Every move of my fingers made a magnified scratching sound on my baby Stella guitar—the guitar, with its mid-range Dobro-like sound, pushed me to new sonic territory. The Lawrence magnetic pickup that the Edge had introduced me to sounded great plugged into my tiny battery-operated Peavey street-busker's amp. The combination was magic—no magnetic-field interference, clear mid-range tone, no buzzing or hum, just pure guitar.

Everything here spoke to an ancient way of life: dirt-floor houses, chickens living inside with the people; the community grinding house for making cornmeal was in the town center. Women walked long distances to the grinding house to crush their corn. The corn they brought looked mutated and dried-out compared to the perfect-smile corn we North Americans are used to from the supermarket.

Nothing was wasted in this tiny village outside Oaxaca. The field workers wore sandals made of rubber car tires, with raw leather ankle straps holding them on to their feet—the result was strangely both biblical and futuristic. In a place like this, nothing gets overlooked. Every piece of string, every berry, every hair had a purpose. It reminded me of my days with my grandmother Aurore. She threw nothing away. Her collected rags made their way into her hand-woven circular carpets, beautiful carpets, made of curious combinations of different-colored scraps. She could even make old panty hose blend in to look pretty, woven alongside discarded rags, T-shirts, pant legs, anything, really.

Her bed quilts were similar; patchwork blends of scraps, beautiful enough to make you cry. We grew up sleeping under these quilts. I wish I had some left, but they were never viewed as collectibles in the environment of need; they all wore out.

I made friends with a farmer across the road. He had never left the village. He wasn't even aware of the other villages nearby. I pointed at the mountain in the distance, on which I could see the little steeple of another village's chapel. My new farmer friend agreed to jump in the car to pay a visit. To his surprise, this new village offered another kind of life; the people there were specialists with color. They collected bugs, berries, and plants of all sorts to make different-color dyes. They had crushed bougainvillea for staining wood, and little black berries that I had never seen for staining wool and hair.

This new village was a little less isolated than its neighbors. Once a week, the dye-makers took their wares to Oaxaca. We followed them down to one of the most amazing open markets I've ever seen, a strange relative to those in Fez, Morocco. It was almost a replication of the Moroccan medina there, but with less defense in its architecture—perhaps these people had not lived with so many invasions. I was unfamiliar with many of the available foods. A curious heap of one food, about seven feet high and as wide as a room, had a hive of people around it, scooping the matter into paper bags. On closer inspection, the heap was in fact made up of millions of grasshoppers cured in cayenne pepper. Where I grew up, a locust storm was a plague. In Oaxaca, it was a source of protein.

The starlit nights, uninterrupted by man-made light, were a profound inspiration for my music. I went deeper and deeper into my open tunings, and my right-hand fingerpicking reached a new level of expertise. I wonder if surgeons operate with the gift of music. I've never stitched arteries back together, but I imagine that the place I had gotten to with my right hand would be similar to where surgeons' hands get.

A man is a man, if a man has a bull. Saturday is the day of rodeo. On that day, the bull does not pull the plow. The men bring their prized possessions to the rodeo, where young teenage boys risk their lives riding the backs of the bulls to test their bravado. The bull is caged in a small corral, where the teenager climbs on it, a single rope wrapped around the animal's belly. The boy spits on the bull, it's cut loose from the corral, and all hell breaks loose. In most cases, the boy is thrown in the air and lands in the mud, the bull mad as hell, ready to kill. The girls are dressed prettily, the mariachi band begins to play—three violins, three horns, upright bass, and guitarrón. The public address system is a single metal horn resembling a megaphone, and there is only one microphone on stage for the featured singer. This little village is one of hundreds, hidden in the hills of Oaxaca.

Every village has a chapel. Every chapel rings its bell at seven in the evening, to signify the end of work. The seven o'clock symphony of bells had a very profound effect on me. I wished that Eno had been there with me to hear this Oaxaca mountains realization of an Eno composition—the randomness of the ringing, chance clusterings of notes, the way the wind was blowing, the frequency of the bell ringers' pull, mixed with the discipline of fixed components, the bells and the villages, which had been there for a long time. They were the long-standing members of the symphony orchestra. It broke my heart when I dropped my recording machine on the floor. My broken tape recorder was not able to document the ringing chapel bells of Oaxaca. I would later go on to simulate the bells. And there is a little piece of them on my record *Here Is What Is*.

Mexico's ancient beauty drew me in, and so I decided that this was where I should make my music. Mainland Mexico was not as geographically friendly as the parts near California, and so I chose to work in Baja. Howard drove an eighteen-wheeler to the "Birdhouse." The Birdhouse, carved in the rock formations of the hills of the Baja Peninsula, not far from Todos Santos, was about to be my home and music-making house for the next year. My drummer friend Brian Blade, my bass player friend Daryl Johnson, and I had just finished a considerable world tour, and I invited them to join me in Mexico so that I could fully tap into the power of our trio. The house was half inside, half outside, a few hundred yards from the Pacific Ocean.

My fascination with the bells was still with me. Down the road from the Birdhouse was a blacksmith's shop. The blacksmith forged and welded metal to accommodate the needs of local farmers. The display of his wares included beautiful handmade cowbells. It was all right there in front of me, the makings of my new cowbell marimba. I went back to the shack to get my guitar tuner. I carefully selected the bells relating to concert pitch. (*Concert pitch* is a term used to refer to an agreed pitch at which all musicians can operate. The European-American concert pitch is A440.) The blacksmith, in fact, had enough bells to cover the entire chromatic scale. My new cowbells were about to become a homemade marimba, built from found objects. This simple idea for building an instrument without a hefty pocketbook belongs to anybody.

This was a great time for my psychedelic music—mostly instrumental, very sonically inventive. Howard was at a peak with sound processing; everyday was a nonstop journey through the labyrinths of experimentation. I was at my weakest then, in terms of my own confidence. Something had happened to me, and I had lost my musical direction. We were very prolific, but something was eluding me; I didn't feel I had anything to hang on to. The very thing I was excited with one day was the thing I'd abandon the next. As I listen to the Birdhouse music now, I feel that my enemy at the time was my self-editing system—so much beauty never released. I'm stronger now, and so the Birdhouse jewels will slowly and surely be released.

Lucy, who cooked for us, had ancient wisdom in her brow. She had nothing, and she was happy.

> Where nobody has and everybody gives.
> There is no sad where death lives, in San Juan.
> Meet me in San Juan, baby I'll be true.
> I will whisper sweet everythings to you.
> Yellow cactus rose, cotton blown by wind,
> beaten brown hands, perfect skin.

The magnetic-field interference that had been my enemy in the recording studio all my life, the buzzing radio frequency interference that had plagued me, was nonexistent in my Mexican studio. The single-coil guitar pickup—the best-sounding guitar pickup made, visible in the Fender Stratocaster (like Jimi Hendrix played)—is also an antenna for magnetic-field interference. Back home in Canada, I couldn't use the single-coil pickup for delicate guitar playing, because the interference was so invasive. The signal-to-noise ratio was not good. But here in Mexico, the signal-to-noise ratio was reversed. They say that high-current power lines and other electrical and electronic communication systems introduce problematic waves into the air. The magnetic-field problems I'd experienced in Los Angeles, Toronto, and other urban crossroads did not exist at the Birdhouse. This rural Pacific coastal town had not been tainted by electro technology.

I checked into a little hotel in Todos Santos to get away from the shop, to regain objectivity about my music. The sweet little hotel was made up of curious hallways, stairs, nooks and cran-

ABOVE: My grandparents; BELOW: (*left to right*) Bob, Ron, and me

ABOVE: Self-styling not recommended; BELOW LEFT: On my Harley 883 about to depart for Florida (© Gilberte Lanois); BELOW RIGHT: My little brother, Ron—even more of a dreamer than me (© Gilberte Lanois)

Danny Lanois who played 53 hours in the marathon.

Ancaster youth in guitar marathon

A 15 year old Ancaster Youth, Danny Lanois, son of Mrs. Jil Lanois, 311 Robina Drive was one of four participants in a guitar marathon which concluded in Hamilton Saturday.

Held at Mel Pallo's Music Studios and Supplies on Parkdale North, the marathon saw 22 year old Fred Vanderwal, Hamilton capture the honors and win a $500 guitar, case and amplifier.

The marathon got underway Wednesday evening, May 24 at 8.30 p.m. It ended at 5.50 p.m. May 27.

Danny dropped out at 8.05 a.m. Saturday morning. A 21 year old Dundas Youth, Gerhard Stegmaier, 56 Mercer Street dropped out at 3.50 p.m. Saturday.

The fourth contestant, 30 year old Barry Walker of Hamilton conceded to Vanderwal.

Vanderwal's record of playing was 61 hours and 55 minutes. The American record was 57 hours and 48 minutes.

OPPOSITE: Homemade console with a start-up button at the left end of the armrest. The button triggered the six-track system. (© Bob Lanois); ABOVE: Me in the basement studio, complete with egg crates (© Bob Lanois)

Nov. 26/1984

Dan Lanois owes a lot to his mom's basement

By MICHAEL QUIGLEY
Special To The Spectator

ALL THE pieces seem to be coming together for Hamilton record producer Dan Lanois.

His latest opus, the co-production of U2's new album, Unforgettable Fire, has been on the charts for the past few weeks. Tickets for the band's Toronto concert at Massey Hall on Dec. 7 sold out within hours.

Another Lanois production credit, the Parachute Club, will be playing Hamilton Place the night before, on Dec. 6. The Parachute Club album — a genuine Canadian smash hit — has already won Lanois a CFNY U-Know award and is nominated for a best production credit for next week's Juno Awards.

IT'S A big step from a basement in Hamilton to a stately home in Ireland. But that's the road travelled by Lanois. The 33-year-old Dan and his 36-year-old brother, Bob, started out in the record producing business 15 years ago, experimenting with odds and ends of recording equipment, assembled in fits and starts and installed in the basement of their mother's home. Today, as co-owners of Grant Avenue Studio in Hamilton, they have an international reputation.

Dan reckons their big breakthrough came "about six years ago, when Brian Eno was living in New York and looking for an inexpensive but high-quality studio."

Eno is a legendary figure — virtually a one-man avant-garde. He

Music, an early innovator in synthesizer/tape-loop developments and the far frontiers of electronic music. Nowadays, in addition to his own series of recordings under the generic title of Ambient Music, Eno is a top-flight record producer, in demand for any number of major recording projects.

Last spring, Island Records commissioned Eno to produce the latest album by the Irish band U2. In turn, Eno engaged Dan Lanois as co-producer and chief engineer for the project. And so, for most of this past summer, Dan was in Ireland, first at Slane Castle and then at Dublin's Windmill Studios.

Eno's clients — or, more accurately, his collaborators (since the resulting records always have a distinctive Eno flavor) — include Talking Heads and David Byrne, and avant-gardists like England's Robert Fripp, Los Angeles pianist Harold Budd and horn player Jon Hassel.

☐ Dan and Bob Lanois at Grant Avenue Studios: True to their roots.

AFTER U2's phenomenally successful North American tour in 1983, the invitation to work with Eno on the production of the latest album was a huge career boost for Lanois.

In a recent interview, Dan described the early stages of the recording with U2 as a combination of rehearsal and live performance. The band set up in the ballroom of Slane Castle, home of their friend, sometime rock promoter and full-time jetsetting aristocrat Lord Mountcharles. The basic instrumental tracks were laid down live,

create "a very loud and open sound." Then, for more intimate tracks and some vocal arrangements, they moved into the adjoining Chinese Room, with more muted acoustics.

Eno and Lanois set up their recording equipment — flown in from New York — in a small drawing room between the ballroom and the Chinese Room. One of Dan's lasting impressions was "the spectacular view of the River Boyne from the drawing room we were using as a studio/control centre."

Describing U2's sound as "very

this album as to recapture "the rawness and energy of the old sound of, say, the early Stones or Beatles albums," Dan believes that the final sound of the album should be "in effect, a live performance captured in the raw."

At the same time, since the New York-supplied recording equipment was "limited, and not really set up for processing, treating and blending," Dan acknowledges that the second half of the project — in Dublin's Windmill Studios — added the "symphonic overtones" which are a U2 hallmark on top of those

THIS IS where the recording process gets complicated, with the addition of the vocal tracks, guitar overdubs, extra instrumental layers — the tricky sound achievements for which bands hire producers like Eno and Lanois.

Although he has worked before with bands who have modified their lyrics in the studio, Dan calls the U2 practice on this album "unlike anything I've ever seen." Lead singer Bono "worked on these lyrics for three weeks, pushing the band to perform and rewriting the lyrics as the tracks developed. It's a very interesting way to work."

As for the content of the new album, Dan describes it as "continuing the concerns and ideas of their last release, War. Bono's been studying the life and work of Martin Luther King recently, and two of the songs are about him." The band members, he adds, don't do "silly love songs. They're into more serious subjects, but they're hoping that the songs are less specific, more open to different interpretations."

This attitude, he believes, comes from the band's relative longevity — they have been together now for six years. "With the loyalty and commitment of the members, there's no way U2 can be called corporate rock 'n' roll. And they have such a sense of history and culture — I suppose that's normal, it seems to be in the air in Ireland."

Dan is convinced that "no amount of producing will overcome a mediocre song or a misdi-

have had the opportunity to work with a band with that sense o commitment.

"There has to be passion," h insists, "the sort of passion that U have for their material."

HAVING ALREADY worke with Eno before the U2 re cording, on the Grant Avenue pro duction of Harold Budd's solo pian album, The Pearl, Dan admits to personal passion for the "atmo spheric or mood music" which ha been Eno's main direction for th past few years.

There is a definite place for thi sort of music, he says, "because it' like a background canvas for you imagination, the musical equiva lent of a landscape."

He says that he had many "inte resting offers of work in London where there's a real rock scene, an much less of the trend-chasin which seems to happen in Canad — more originality and invention. However, nothing was settled dur ing the European trip.

Back in Hamilton, and fired b his status as co-producer on the U record, he's considering his othe love, "for grooves and dance mu sic."

One plan is "to spend a month i New York, just to get into the danc ing, to soak up the sounds in th clubs and think about the possibili ty of making a really great danc record."

What makes a good producer Why did Eno and U2 and Islan Records want Dan Lanois along fo this record?

LEFT: Advertising poster designed by my brother Bob to drum up a little business (© Bob Lanois); OPPOSITE: Malcolm Burn and me in the magnificent New Orleans control room (© Bob Lanois)

OPPOSITE: With Billy Bob in Toronto (© Jennifer Tipoulow); ABOVE: Brian Eno and me posing for the camera at Slane Castle (© Colm Henry); BELOW: Party picture—Bono and me

Recording with the Neville Brothers. Howard looking twelve years old, me looking eighteen (© Christine Alicino)

LEFT: *Time Out of Mind* album cover, shot at the Teatro
(© Daniel Lanois)

BELOW: A light moment during the Willie Nelson session, at the Teatro
(© Danny Clinch)

Willie Nelson and Emmylou Harris at the Teatro (© Donata Wenders)

Me and Willie at the Teatro (© Donata Wenders)

With my buddy Robbie Robertson (© Danny Clinch)

RIGHT: Neil Young and me in the kitchen (© Keisha Kalfin); BELOW: Chris Whitley and me, in Austin, Texas (© Danny Clinch)

ABOVE: My church in a suitcase (© Donata Wenders); BELOW: The aftermath of a moment of anger (© Keisha Kalfin)

nies, secret passages, and beautiful tropical gardens. I lived on the top floor, a humble small apartment with rooftop access. The symphony of Todos Santos was different than the Oaxaca bell symphony; where I grew up, the rooster would start its call with the sunrise, but the Todos Santos roosters were the "up all night" variety, and the dogs did not need much encouragement to join them. I eventually got used to the Dog and Rooster Symphony, but it stood in stark contrast to the otherwise tranquil nature of the place.

My hotel bedroom had one of the most beautiful multicolored floors I'd ever seen. On a close inspection, I realized that it was in fact a simple cement slab that had had a design pressed into it before it dried. When I asked the locals how it was done, they showed me a tool that resembled a metal cookie cutter, but was twelve inches square with a long handle on it; the design was a floral pattern, a bit like decorative wrought-iron work. With the aid of a geometrical plumb line, the floor layer would press the cookie cutter into the still wet cement, creating a repeating tile pattern across the entire floor. Once the cement was dry, an artist would hand-paint every leaf, every vine, and every detail of the impression with the most beautiful array of colors. What would otherwise have been a plain concrete slab had now been turned into a blazing floral work of art.

This cost-effective way of creating beauty reminded me of the floors of my childhood back in Quebec; also driven by lack of funds, my Quebec relatives proved imaginative and resourceful. A country house in Quebec, needing a fresh floor, received an installation called a Prelart. The Prelart, simply the cheapest linoleum flooring available, often a drab color, was usually laid down by the man of the house and his friends. The women of the house would then enhance it, hand-painting a random floral pattern onto the surface. Their work made it beautiful, not only by their choices of motif and shape, but by their homespun dedication. The painted motif eventually fades as the paint on the Mexican floor does, but the wear and tear is all part of the beauty.

I would have liked to stay longer in Mexico, but the calendar caught up to me, and I found myself on a plane to Berlin to fulfill my commitment to U2 and Eno. We were starting U2's new record, *Achtung Baby.* The wall had just come down, and Berlin was a hive of activity—money coming into the city, people migrating this way and that way, celebrating their newfound freedom. Renegade roadside markets sprang up selling all kind of objects that looked strange to my Canadian eye: bits and pieces of antiquated military equipment, winter clothing from another time. I lived in a hotel on the east side of Berlin, but Hansa Studios, where we were working, was just on the west side of where the wall had existed. That very large complex, complete with a handsomely designed old orchestra room, was about to be the birthplace of *Achtung Baby.*

The U2 artillery had arrived before me. The orchestra room was fully equipped with band gear and a complete, sophisticated live-performance mixing console that would be used to provide stage-monitor and headphone blends for the band members, Eno, and me. The control room was down the hall; communication was via camera. This is always challenging, but we felt that the inspiring orchestra room was fair-enough compensation for the discomfort of separating our recording crew from the performance crew; and besides, we had Joe O'Herlihy in charge of running the monitor console. Joe has been mixing live sound for U2 since the eighties. He is not only the best at his work; he is a rock-solid individual and a dear friend. Flood, who had engineered U2's *The Joshua Tree*, had agreed to be at the helm in the Berlin control room. This was great news, as we had the winning team fully intact. Our hearts were burning with desire. We were in a rare creative position; massive commercial success under the belt, reinventing rock 'n' roll in our dreaming minds. We all wanted to make a masterpiece.

The mountain villages of Oaxaca had offered me the symphony of the bells, and Todos Santos had brought me the symphony of dogs and roosters. Now Berlin was bringing me the streetcar train symphony. The hotel was a stone's throw from a cul-de-sac that marked the end of the trains' journey through the city. As the trains turned, their wheels made a beautiful symphonic sound. Every cold winter morning, armed with my now-repaired Sony tape recorder, I took the time to record the symphonic sounds of wheels squealing their high-pitched melodies at the end point of their route. The primal metal cries were beautiful to me. Perhaps part of the beauty was the state of mind that staying quiet in one place, say for one hour without moving, brings. I had felt this feeling before back in Canada, when Eno and I went to the bird lands to record the symphony of birds as the sun rose outside Hamilton, Ontario. To sit with a friend and say nothing for an hour is an experience I would recommend to all. It's a relative of meditation, I'm sure; a time for the mind to slow down and empty itself.

These early Berlin recordings of trains let my mind go to faraway places that I should probably revisit in my current busy times. Berlin was cold and harsh, so why were we there? U2 wanted to make a record that had European rock 'n' roll flavor. David Bowie had worked in Hansa Studios in the seventies and made great records, coincidentally with Eno. Now, twenty years later, Eno was standing in the same room he had stood in with Bowie and Iggy Pop. Rumor has it they shared lodging at that time as well. It must have been quite a creative force—Iggy Pop with his punk wild ways, Bowie with his imagination and charisma, and Eno at the height of his seventies sonic experiments.

We found a cool old drum kit in the closet of Hansa, a set of Sonars from the sixties. Larry Mullen first played them for kicks, but then kept playing them as we realized that in fact they were great recording drums. This little pearl white kit pretty much dominated the drum corner for the rest of *Achtung Baby.* Larry had gotten really great on the drums by this point, and to this day, I love listening to *Achtung Baby,* largely due to the drumming energy. The song "You're So Cruel" is a fine example of where we had gotten the drums to; a throwback to the funk drum sounds of the early seventies, surrounded by futuristic electro.

Adam Clayton was still using his throaty Ampeg SVT sound then, and I have to say, it's fucking great. Adam has evolved to a deeper bass sound, but in recent conversation, we decided that it might be nice to pull out the snarly old Clayton sound for a few numbers.

Flood and I spent a lot of days treating the beats of *Achtung Baby.* This was all before digital technology's ease of operation, and so there were many late sessions of us jockeying drums around from take to take, to fully optimize Larry's best playing. All kinds of echo manipulations were applied. In fact, the entire album was dominated by sound experiments. Between Eno, Flood, the Edge, and me, there was never a moment where we weren't pushing the sonic envelope.

As I hear that record now, I am mystified about how it all happened. Bono was at a turning point in his lyrics, during which the complexities of life and human emotion fueled him to write new kinds of songs. He wanted songs that showed the dark side of love as much as the beauty. The song "Love Is Blindness" addresses the issue of someone being driven by an ideal to the point of contaminating the very fiber of his morals. The song "One" was born in Berlin, a song of hope that talks about how differences of opinion should not block the way to higher levels of friendship and communication. Misassumption is often the enemy of admiration. Talk to someone, let him in and learn what he is about. Your differences may not matter once you have a relationship.

By this point with U2, Eno and I were very welcome to play our instruments and be guest members of the band. Wherever it made sense, we were happy to lend a musical hand. Eno and I have always played well together, and that's what we like to do once all the planning and philosophizing goes quiet. For me, the song "One" has echoes of "I Still Haven't Found What I'm Looking For" built into it. I embraced it with all my love and might. It was one of those songs that stands outside of an artist's control; it lives because it needs to. My prunings and contributions to "One" were steady and driven by care.

During one of our morning sessions, Eno and I provided a mantra repeating-line melody. It was a Les Paul and unison synthesizer, blues-based part, like something you might hear on an old Muddy Waters record. It stands as a constant in the tapestry of guitar parts, acting as the dividing line between two sides of a story. Like the flow of a river dividing two sides of a city. A later guitar part, the hammer-on guitar at the beginning of the song, is a part I played at Bono's request. Could you play a little something, Danny? Bono always likes to hear a fresh ingredient to inspire a vocal take. My little hammer-on made the finish line. The Edge's chord sequences are beautiful. As I study the song "One" now, I hear the sophistication of the Edge's chordal twists and turns, ghostly shifting with Bono's emotional turns in the lyrics. Sometimes I wonder if we are all driven by premonition and instinct. God bless mystery.

It's been said that Berlin was a tough emotional time for all of us, but I remember it as a time of search for direction. There's nothing wrong with searching; the worst that can happen is that it may make you feel lost, but when you find something special after a long search, the reward will be all the greater.

Record production has always been a feeding ground for me. If I do good work on someone's record, I come back to mine with a belly full of confidence and ideas, the power of osmosis. The Birdhouse setup was still intact when I returned to Mexico. Howard was in a good place with his sounds, and when he had to go back to Canada, my old friend Wayne Lorenz, who has been very supportive of my music, took over as engineer. Wayne still crosses through my world today. We're currently working together on a project, restoring a Toronto Buddhist temple as my new Canadian shop.

Most of the offers that come my way I have to say no to, oftentimes because of schedule congestion, but there are some invitations that you simply have to say yes to. Would Lanois like to record his own version of a Leonard Cohen song? Yes, I said, and I chose "The Stranger." This song had been a favorite of mine forever, and so I huddled up the band to build a rendition in the Birdhouse Mexican environment.

Capitol Records was behind this compilation project. Many artists had been invited to make contributions, and so I was honored and very happy that they let me have a go at "The Stranger." I found my way into "The Stranger" perhaps by having been one myself. We're all strangers to somebody. I've always questioned the phrase "Don't talk to any strangers." What might be reasonable advice to a child walking home from school might not be good life advice. I've met the most wonderful people through chance encounters, people with the most amazing life stories that I would not have heard if I had kept cautiously to myself. I've been hurt a few times, but the enrichment that has come to me by trusting people could never be replaced.

Daryl Johnson came in with a wonderful melodic bass line, and Brian Blade played a dark rolling tom-tom figure. This new "Stranger" had found its own magic, and I couldn't wait to play it for Leonard. On the outskirts of Hancock Park in Los Angeles, I knocked on Leonard's door. Leonard greeted me with a platter and asked if I wanted any chopped liver. His place was simple, and felt like home—various bits of furnishings from different eras. I accepted a glass of wine, as Leonard listened to my version of "The Stranger" on my Walkman headphones. I was nervous because I had left out two verses to try and bring the song in at a reasonable length. Leonard removed the headphones, and said it was the best rendition of any of his songs for this project he had heard. I apologized for having left out two verses. He said don't worry, it's all fine, as long as there's some mention of "The Stranger" somewhere. The mysterious visit faded, and as I write this, I feel like it might have even been a mirage. I was given the axe by some head at Capitol Records, and my recording of "The Stranger" never got included in the compilation; but I'd do it all again for a chopped-liver evening with Leonard.

My time in Mexico ran out, and Howard drove the eighteen-wheeler back to the States. When you move this much equipment around, you have to deal with brokers that issue licenses called carnets. My carnet had expired, and so off to California, to the house of "Desert Fred" in Joshua Tree. Desert Fred looked after my equipment, and I got to use his house. When I wasn't there, he was welcome to do his own recordings. The bleakness of the desert appealed to me. Sometimes the loudest sound was a fly buzzing around the room. I put my speakers on the roof of my car, and blasted the Joshua Tree canyon with my new recordings—I loved it, but my insecurities were still with me. Running to a new location had not made me more decisive. Howard was also messed up in the head; he disappeared for a while. Everything ground to a halt, and I didn't know who I was. The motorcycle was the only thing I felt connected to.

11

THE SAUSAGE STAND AT THE ECHO

My friend Jennifer Tefft invited me to go to the Echo. Jennifer books bands in Silverlake at a club called Spaceland, and is also associated with the Echo. The two clubs promote all kinds of mixtures of live music. On the right night, on Jennifer's cue, I roll down with my customized motorcycle, twenty-one-inch counterweighted wheel and all, to catch a glimpse of what other people are doing. A lot of what I hear there is not industry fed. It is driven by hungry hearts and the love of music. A recent Spaceland visit exposed me to the beautiful singing of Rocco Deluca, a blues-based futurist accompanied by a traditional Brazilian cajón, which is a sit-down drum with a deep sound. A thousand yards from my bed in Silverlake, I heard Rocco's commitment and it touched me—inspired me to keep pushing the envelope of my own music.

Farther down the boulevard is the Echo. Along the filthy sidewalk, under a concrete bridge, five hundred people are lined up to get into the back door of the club for a night of transformation, young people looking to be lifted out of their skins. Tefft and I join the line to the Echo, with the aroma of sausages cooking under the bridge. The health department is not here to give a rating to the sausage-stand operation. The operators are not static enough to ever be tagged.

South-of-the-border folks, Guatemalan or Mexican perhaps, see the sidewalk vending as a livelihood, cooking sausages and onions on a cold Echo Park night. There is something Republican about them. They're hardworking family people, making cash to feed their kids and send them to school. Somewhere up on a hill, a fortunate established white perspective sees them as illegal border jumpers. But what kind of person drags equipment to the roadside under a concrete bridge in Echo Park to cook sausages and onions late into the night? Someone who wants a better life and is willing to work hard for it. Abiding by the Ten Commandments, if not the local bylaw, the sausage-stand people have everything in them that the early American spirit embraced. The sausages steamed; the Echo Park clubgoers, unstoppable with their appetite for music (and sausages), were beautiful.

This congregation under the concrete bridge did not exist two years ago, but somebody had rolled the dice on the Eastside. Let's use "Eastside" as a figure of speech for the bad neighborhood with affordable rents. The rise of the Eastside is driven by economy. The more established expensive neighborhoods don't attract newcomers without cash, therefore these newcomers must go to the affordable Eastside. And that's how it starts—the rise of a new scene.

People starting out, dreamers, really—dreaming of owning a club, a shop, or just having an apartment—all begin coming to the Eastside. Soon, what was regarded as a dangerous place that you wouldn't want to go to, becomes cool. The little shops are innovative, new designers, etc. Coffee shops pop up, the restaurants get good, and it all becomes more interesting than the tired, "seen it all before," more rich but used-up tourist hood. Perhaps the term "Birth of the Cool" applies. This is not happening just because people are cool. It's happening because of economics.

Memories of the Riverboat come to mind. The Riverboat was a tiny club in Toronto, a crossroads for a lot of great touring music artists of the sixties and seventies. Joni Mitchell played there, Dylan and all kinds of folkies comin' up waltzed through the Riverboat. I used to play there myself as a young guitar player. The vibe was well established, silence was expected at show time. There was depth, humor, and respect. A good night at the Riverboat promised a lasting experience that equaled the experience of having read an interesting book.

The Red Devils motorcycle club operated on the next block. Nimbus 9 recording studio—host to Alice Cooper and the Guess Who, and where Peter Gabriel made his first solo album—was on the other block. Head shops, leatherworkers, and clothes makers were all part of the cultural revolution. It was the hippest place in Toronto.

How do you keep a cool village going without the franchise-driven mentality muscling in to bring it all down to the lowest common denominator? The Village in Toronto is still around, but records aren't being made there. The Riverboat is gone, as are the bikers. You have to be rich to keep an apartment, and if you can't afford nine hundred dollars a night at the Four Seasons, or can't afford to clothe yourself in designer wear, then you're out. That's fine, but it will not be a welcome mat to the new wave of artistic and innovative minds. They are going to the Eastside.

There are those of us who do not appreciate Jamba Juice butted up against Target, butted up against Taco Bell, butted up against Burger King, with condos on top. The Eastside is made of hopes and dreams, and I like it. The Silverlake Eastside has a motorcycle customization shop that just popped up, with two guys in it that are great; they're part of an aesthetic awareness that is catching on—some kind of synchronicity at play—where people are more aware of lines, lines of design. Referencing the seventies in search of a classic, related somehow to the sampling of music from another time. The contemporary motorcycle engines, brakes, and general moving-part efficiency is better than ever, but the lines of the seventies are not to be forgotten. These young motorcycle customizers are futurists who also embrace the classics.

The Eastsiders are enjoying the luxury of postmodern times. They want to make improvements and not just have straight-out-of-the-box stock looks. The same way that Eno will devote a year of his life to the building of his own sounds on a synthesizer. He also doesn't like things straight out of the box. He likes his own creations to be his sonics, and we love him for that. That's why he's Eno. There wouldn't be an Eno if he had surrendered to the commonplace. He is a customizer of sound, a transformer of rooms, a chaser of ideas, a fighter for beauty—he is a futurist. He is a living example of his own philosophy, a modifier like I try to be.

I can remember standing in a club in New York City circa 1985, listening to the Fat Boys, a rare and inventive trio. Acrobatic sounds came from their mouths into a stage microphone, providing their rhythms—a human beat box, essentially, with poetry and prose riding over top. It was the first chapter of rap. From the street, from the hearts of these young men, a sound and expression had risen up, a sound that had nothing to do with the usual artillery of rock 'n' roll. They were flesh and bone and three microphones. They had decided to customize.

I suppose the moral of the story is that of resourcefulness. God bless the hearts of the Fat Boys and anyone willing to roll the dice on the Eastside—including the sausage makers under the concrete bridge.

12

EMMYLOU HARRIS

On motorcycles, the counterweight on the twenty-one-inch wheel is an afterthought that helps achieve a perfectly balanced wheel. It looks like a little piece of lead stuck on the rim of a wheel, placed there by a dedicated mind to ensure that the motorcycle does not start wobbling at higher speed. Records are that way to me—I don't like them to wobble at high speed. I want their balance and finely tuned harmonic structure to resonate in the high winds of time. I want the voice of Emmylou Harris to touch hearts, even if it is excavated from a postapocalyptic, postnuclear tar pit in the year 3007. This state of microscopy is a condition that I am happy to live with, if it means I can make better records.

The call came through my office, and I was sent a cassette recording of Emmylou Harris demonstrating a few song choices for her up-and-coming album *Wrecking Ball*. Emmy had noticed and liked my solo record *Acadie*, as well as my many productions on other peoples' records. The simplicity of her recording touched me. I heard the frailty inside the confidence of this master singer's voice. I had grown up listening to Emmy, and in fact some of her past work had been a point of reference for me as a steel guitar player. You couldn't be a steel player and not know "Love Hurts" (sung by Emmy and Gram Parsons), for example. There was a whole movement happening in the seventies that Emmy had been part of—country music meeting rock 'n' roll, really, with the likes of Neil Young rising through the ranks of Buffalo Springfield and Crosby, Stills and Nash. Agreeing to meet Emmylou, I found myself in Nashville on a rainy night, waiting for her to pick me up from a hotel. The plan was to go back to her place and listen to some music. She picked me up in a Jeep (stick shift, basic model), and halfway to her house she hit the ditch and just about rolled us over. In her defense, the ditch had filled with water and could easily have been mistaken for a puddle (I took a cab back). We made it to the house okay, and I met the entire Harris clan.

The house trembled with the dignity of American values that I have not felt very often. Decency and compassion were there at every turn, photos and collectibles of historical family significance in every room. Emmy's father had been a pilot in the war, and there was a quiet pride in his photographic presence. I had felt this atmosphere in other houses growing up, houses where ancestry was intact. Where books had been kept and wisdom passed on. Where folk-music collections made it possible to trace sources of inspiration. Some small back shelf might contain the secret Peruvian melody adapted by a young Jewish hopeful in the fifties, fascinated with the bohemian life of New York City. The kinds of shelves that Paul Simon and Bob Dylan might have rummaged through, looking to absorb the richness of story, melody, and song.

In this house, I felt the presence of Johnny Cash, Dolly Parton, Gram Parsons, Linda Ronstadt, the Carter Family, and George Jones—like the ghosts that had looked down upon me, as guardians on the Nevilles' project. But this was a new set of ghosts, new guardians for the making of *Wrecking Ball*. I felt deep American patriotism in the walls of Emmy's home, and I was humbled by the unspoken dedication to values that I had never known. These were highly intelligent people whose opinions on important matters of freedom, American foreign policy, and fundamental humanitarian rights I could trust. Emmy's house made me sad some, too; sad that I had never come up in this kind of privileged, informative, intellectual environment. Where I had grown up, this kind of access to information belonged only to the rich.

I knew I was going to produce a record for Emmy five minutes into my visit to her house. As always, I was attracted to the unknown. Her life journey and experiences were about to jump on me. I knew I would come out of this project with valuable knowledge. We listened to various records and song choices that Emmy liked. Yes, I listened, but mostly I fantasized. When a vibe jumps on me, it triggers my imagination. I was already putting a band together, a band that would represent tradition and yet give Emmy a chance to broaden her scope. I made a decision that I would build a record guided by Emmy's emotional makeup. Records ring true when they represent the emotional position of an artist.

The usual record company enthusiasm was around, lots of handshaking, one big happy family. Nice folks and all, but I had seen it all before, and it didn't make a stick of difference to me. I knew what it took to deliver the goods. You can place a bet on a boxer and slap him on the back, then sponge him down and fill him with bravado and instruction. But when the bell rings, those faces on the other side of the ropes are a blur. The punches come and you dodge them, or you may take them full on—all the endorsements and promises become insignificant, and as the sweat rolls off of your face, you punch like a madman and fight with every ounce for what you believe in. Life flashes by in front of you, years of Travis Picking study, of memorizing sequences and arrangements. "The Tennessee Waltz" cheers you on; "The Tennessee Stud" rides by. Choruses of men hauling iron ore shout out, "I owe my soul to the company store." You can hear them tear down Darlin' Corey's "Still House" as Jimi Hendrix demands to be considered a folk hero alongside Pete Seeger and Woody Guthrie, as civil rights goes into battle headed by generals—Muhammad Ali, John Coltrane, Elvin Jones, Sister Rosa, James Brown, the Temptations, Stevie Wonder—generals fighting with the ultimate weapon, excellence. Excellence lived in Emmylou's house. I felt privileged to be invited to the table.

I decided I was going to build a classic. The overwhelming sensation that I have felt at every moment of great decision rode over me like a wave; I was going in and I would not let up until we were there. What resources did I have that I could apply? Larry Mullen on the drums, yes. Larry loves country music, and every part that he plays sounds deep. I don't know where his thing comes from, but Larry sounds deep and he is deep, and I don't even want to know where it comes from, not yet. I'm happy to receive his playing as a gift, and to get his thing on as many records as he wants to be on with me. Larry Mullen, whom I've known for twenty-five years, and who I still don't know.

I invited Malcolm Burn to engineer and play piano, and to also play his usual electro keyboards at the console, much like we had done for Dylan. Malcolm and I play well together. We hit on a blend of honky-tonk piano and electric mandolin, and the haunting harmonic interplay between these two instruments became part of the sound of *Wrecking Ball*, sometimes further embellished by dulcimers that I had picked up at Emmy's house. The multiple strings of these instruments ringing in unison created a harmonic cohesion, a sort of choral group, moving with every chord change. A symphony of Appalachian instruments,

"Wrecking Ball" is harmonious and rich, largely due to this discovery.

A strange and beautiful balance was struck on this album. The sound of some of my favorite records from the sixties had just appeared in front of me, like a dream come true, like a fantasy never realized coming into reality. I felt that I had a chance to make a record as spine-chilling as Phil Spector's production of the Crystals, featuring Darlene Love, coincidentally one of Emmy's heroes. Of course I was at a great advantage; I had Emmylou Harris in the room. Her flawless live vocals became the last leaf falling onto a fall harvest.

It was all there, all that family history, those deeply rooted American values, Appalachian memories, echoes of ancient Irish melodies giving comfort to the brave new pioneers settling in the mountains of America. Canadians are a strange breed, with a dogged capacity to curate and trace sources. Burn and I became guardians of Emmylou. The production of *Wrecking Ball* started in Nashville, and then moved down to New Orleans, all members of the cast living in my house. There was no escape.

"Wrecking Ball" is the title of a Neil Young song that we decided to include on Emmy's record. A cool track had been cut, complete with heavy Larry Mullen tom-toms. Against all odds, Neil Young flew into New Orleans on a private jet and selflessly gave his all to our project. When he arrived, we played him our version of "Wrecking Ball." He rose to his feet and slow-danced with his wife, Pegi, who had joined him on this trip. I was touched and took it as a sign that Neil approved of our rendition. Neil sat at my Steinway B and worked up a harmony for the song. He then added a harmonica and also sang background on "Sweet Old World"; it was all kind of surreal. There I was one more time, the Canadian kid surrounded by his heroes. The bottom end of the record had been well covered by Tony Hall, whom

I had worked with on the Nevilles' record, and who had also played the memorable bass line on my own song "The Maker." Lucinda Williams and Steve Earle had kindly stopped by and lent their charisma to their songs chosen for *Wrecking Ball.* Lucinda had written "Sweet Old World" and Steve had written "Goodbye."

Emmylou has had a long-standing friendship with the McGarrigle Sisters. These great Canadian singers have a beautiful and special blend, a sort of warbling bird sound. The sisters traveled to New Orleans to sing on a few selections, including their own song "Goin' Back to Harlan," which we'd cut a version of. Their egoless dedication reminded me of what group singing is all about: blend. It's not a time to stand out; it's a time of consideration for others. Even in the absence of a lyric, a blend can cause a listener to feel emotion, it can speak to us, take us to a higher state. The McGarrigles with Emmylou—that is a higher state. Daryl Johnson, my old friend and a master falsetto singer, stopped in and sang some spine-chilling top parts, high up above Emmy—what a sound. There's something wonderful about a man singing above a woman.

My brother Bob was filming the entire process, and managed to pull off a cool video of Emmylou in my lush garden. Bob also did the artwork for the cover, and the documentary that he shot called *Building the Wrecking Ball* pretty much tells the whole story. It was all adding up to soul music—generous input was supplied by all. *Wrecking Ball* won a Grammy Award, and is already considered to be a classic.

The French Quarter was alive with action as the hipster zone was expanding all the way over to Frenchmen Street. Café Brasil, run by my Brazilian friend Ade, was jumping every night, all kinds of bands playing there. In fact, that's where I first heard Brian Blade play when I was out on a walk with Iggy Pop. Perhaps my instinct had been right when I had built my studio in New Orleans. Bohemian life was high, and once again I felt that I was in the heart of a significant movement and scene.

After a fruitful chapter, it all came to an end. For personal reasons I moved to Mexico and eventually sold the house. That was it for New Orleans, but from the bottom of my heart, I can say that I gave that city my all. Storms come and go, as people come and go. We are all mini-hurricanes and perhaps I would not have gone to New Orleans at all if Hurricane Katrina had already happened. But I hope that if one was to add up all the albums recorded in New Orleans, relative to my being there, one might see a ripple in the Mississippi River—Bob Dylan paddling alongside Louis Armstrong, the Neville Brothers alongside Billie Holiday, Pearl Jam alongside Lee Dorsey, R.E.M. alongside the Dixie Cups, maybe Danny Lanois alongside Leo Nocentelli. A little Canadian ripple, like a piece of ice, that somehow floated all the way down to the Gulf of Mexico.

One final sad part of leaving the city was having to let go of my collection of Harley-Davidsons. My friend Big Al from Texas came by with a truck, handed me a big bag of cash, and drove all the bikes away. I haven't seen Al for a while.

Bye-bye, New Orleans.

13

THE ONE-POINT SOURCE

My first band could afford only one guitar amplifier. In fact, it belonged to the bass player, Mau. Mau's amp was a cute little one-volume-knob, three-input-jacks, eight-inch-speaker National; the first input for the bass, the second for the guitar, and the third for the singer's microphone. The National amp was our entire public address system. The eight-inch speaker did its best to project; we were a democracy controlled by the dictatorship of a suffocating speaker. The speaker did its best to accommodate the transients, the sudden loud sounds that momentarily poked out to feature a dynamic moment, as expressed by the musicians. Not all expressions at once, only the loudest expression at a given moment.

This technological limitation offered something beautiful. A one-point source is a dynamic delivery of a group effort. In its primal way, it did away with competition. Think of the many times that you've seen a band live, and you can't hear the singer because somebody else is playing too loud. Too many mics, too many pieces of equipment might put all instruments on the same plane, but it can create mumbo jumbo. I like the idea of a one-point source, not only in a guitar amplifier, but in a human delivery. Some of my favorite recordings that I've done have been a snapshot of an already well-balanced group of musicians and singers; Emmylou Harris's *Wrecking Ball* qualifies as an example. The instruments in the room were never louder than the singing. The human source was balanced such that even one single mono microphone would still give the listener pleasurable and balanced listening. Get your source right, and your end will be right.

I was recently impressed by a Blind Willie Johnson recording. That very old recording gave me the sensation of a one-point source. It felt like I was standing in front of Blind Willie Johnson, rather than listening to a record. There was a darkness in the guitar, a warble in the voice, but the two ingredients had unity. These two sounds were blended by the performance environment, i.e., by the room or the back porch or by the weather, and not by the multimicrophone, multitracking separation-of-ingredients technique that is the norm of our contemporary times. I believe the human ear finds comfort in these more snapshotlike, technically noncomplex recordings, like the human eye finds comfort in a movie scene that is shot with one camera. The single camera pans across the room, relative to the action, the same way that our human eye moves to explore a scene, relative to its point of interest. The opposite would be fast edits to multiple camera angles. Fast edits may create excitement, but staying with one camera for an extended time will make what you see believable. The long-lasting single-camera shot is a philosophy that I recently tried to exercise in the making of the *Here Is What Is* film, which is made up of camera documentation of my work in various studios over the course of a year. The resulting feeling is one of looking through someone's diary—musical-performance-room action vs. film-editing-room action.

Think of the comfort of the kitchen radio. A recent visit to a friend's restaurant reinforced my one-point-source philosophy. He couldn't afford a big sound system, and so he had only a small blaster on his open kitchen counter. A lack of funds might have led to a stroke of genius. The cook got to be the DJ. The cook, who is obviously in tune with the action of the room, plays what he wants at the volume that he wants on a nice little blaster. A simple one-point-source device provided a cozy kitchen sensation for my friend's one-room restaurant. Much like sitting around a fireplace, sitting by a simple little blaster can provide warmth and comfort. A quick reach for the volume knob makes for an adjustment relative to the demands of the room. That would be hard to pull off if one had to run down the hall to adjust racks of amplifiers, crossovers, and graphic equalizers designed to make the cook feel inadequate. Give me a Blaupunkt mono one-point-source radio out of a 1972 Mercedes and I'm happy.

The one-point source continues. Imagine eight people in a phone booth—they would certainly have to get along. The summing amplifier is a sort of phone booth; it's a collecting place for sounds. You can think of it like a final stage of congregation before songs make it to a record, much like the little National amplifier of my first band. The summing amplifier will respond the best it can to the sound information it is sent. If you send a lot of bass to the summing amp, and then also send it high-frequency information like a mandolin, the amplifier may have trouble handling both signals. Consequently, it will favor one or the other depending on the dynamic action, and here we have it again—a self-mixing system. The more tracks we use in recording (Pro Tools, for example), the further away we get from the help of the summing amp.

How did the Beatles ever do it in the sixties with only four tracks? They combined a group of instruments to a summing amplifier and committed to that blend, to a single track. The limitation of the summing amplifier was now carved in stone. Come mixing time, the pushing of a single fader might give you 50 percent of the sound of your record. Adding equalization, compression, or filtering to that group of instruments now living on a single track will fast bring about personality results, based on the decision that you can't change your mind about—marriage without the escape of divorce.

Shirley doesn't ask for more
She works at the diner
She mops the floor
Her baby said momma
I'm gonna buy you a mountain
Momma said you can't own a mountain
You can sit on it for a while

She said baby I know
I know it's getting late
You have broken through walls
Through so many gates
But there is one that I think you've missed
Its evil iron is shattered by a kiss
The acquisitions keep coming in
Till the brain bags out the skin
Till the fingers don't know how to touch
And the heart beats double-dutch
She said baby I know it's hard to stop
Cause your engine drive is the drug that you've got
Some kind of nomad blood won't let you rest
Some kind of nomad blood running through your chest
But I want you
But I want you like a turbo wants a charge

Momma's milk never wanted this
Drop that sword and swallow her kiss
I will love you in the presence of doubt
I will love you when there's no food for your mouth
Give up the ghost that won't let you go
You've got to get out before you're sick you know
Sirens ringing on the hotel window
Dreams dried up of wheat and silo
The bass drum pounds the load of a dusty road ahead
And another strangled heart lying sad on a bed
You want to be special
You want to know dark and din
But your stomach is sinking for fame
A taste of win
I'm coming to you like a runaway train
Coming to you like ancient refrain
Coming to you to dominate the money
And be your sweet soul honey
Sweet honey
Sweet honey
Sweet honey
Sweet honey

14

TIME OUT OF MIND

Bob Dylan read me the lyrics to *Time Out of Mind* in a hotel room in New York City. He asked if I thought we had a record, and I said yes. I hadn't heard a note or any melody, but an overwhelming sensation came over me. I was stunned by the power of the lyrics. Bob had written from a perspective that few had seen. Decades of life experience and testimony lay on the pages in front of me. The myth that rock 'n' roll belonged only to youth was about to be shattered by the steel blue eyes of the man himself. The darkness of the lyric was even darker than me.

I left with inspiration and a list of records that Bob recommended as good rock 'n' roll references: Charlie Patton, Little Walter, Arthur Alexander, and others. I listened to these records and I understood. I understood that the technology that existed in the forties and fifties was not meant to handle rock 'n' roll. The preamplifiers of that era were built for distant miking, for symphonic or big-band applications. When rock 'n' roll arrived, it overdrove those preamps, pushing the gear beyond the manufacturer's recommended use. The birth of this great new medium called rock 'n' roll was afforded the luxury of *overdrive.*

Bob wanted that sound, and I felt I knew how to get it. As a kid I had experienced the back end of that era. My own studio in Canada had suffered from those same problems, too much level for the microphone preamps to handle. The result is overdrive, a nice quality for rock 'n' roll. The rebel stance of the era was challenging the medium. We like being naughty—that's what kids do, they do what their parents didn't do. New discoveries on the horizon—a new birth with the old dogs under your arm, like a stack of classic books. You're not gonna rewrite the same book, but you're gonna be smart enough to at least read through it. Relevance is content measured up against the past. Bob wanted relevance, and I vowed to give it to him.

Bob and I had gone the distance back in '88 on his record *Oh Mercy*, and his description of it all in his book *Chronicles* is pretty accurate. I couldn't disagree with any of it; perhaps the chronology was different than I remembered. That was New Orleans, and we were different people back then. They say that every cell in the body regenerates every seven years. The racehorse that I used to be was now a workhorse. My guitar playing, and for that matter, my understanding of the blues, had come a long way.

Oh Mercy was built on a chance encounter; I wasn't supposed to make a record with Bob Dylan. I was just pushing my thing around, like a big ball of soft snow. The incredible weight building at every roll, that crunching you hear as you push your shoulder into a ball that weighs five hundred pounds, every roll picking up more snow until you stare at the result of the momentum. What had I built? A rolling stone gathers no moss; the big ball of snow that I had rolled from Canada had done the opposite. This big heavy ball had everything rolled into it. Bits of leaves mixed with temptation, regret covered up by generosity, the dying breed of significant content gasping for air as the ball rolled. Bob came around and hooked in; he didn't know what I was about, but he knew I wasn't about to let him down—because I cared.

There is a difference between admiring something from a distance and being in it. Every now and again, something rises out of the ground overnight, like a mushroom, or like a vine growing on a concrete bridge—no soil, just growing—and you wonder how it even happened. One little seed in the wind catches in a crack and it starts—nothing to do with planning. The vine creeps, and it might just become the very thing that eventually holds up the bridge. Bob had been that vine before, I knew he could be again. I didn't mind tropical nights, storms—whatever Louisiana had to offer was fine by me. Perhaps some of my ancestors were already down here, my skin color was right; I could read their signs, I knew what *Pontchartrain* meant. The buzzing wires, rats swaggin' on poles, cypress trees whispering the same song they had always whispered. "Snowball Lanois" in Louisiana. Sometimes things are just the way they are.

Bob had been wearing a hood for a long time, like a boxer keeping warm before the first round. I liked watching his face, that hood flapping in the midnight New Orleans air. I wasn't gonna be there for long, but what I was about to do was gonna be there after I was gone. But that was *Oh Mercy*, it was the past, and now we were about to make *Time Out of Mind*.

No matter where you are or who you are, you're only ever gonna sit in a chair and sing your song or play your guitar if somebody wants to hear you. The publicists may have had a go at building up your legend, or the journalists might have spun the yarns about your significance, but all that is nothing but oil floating on top of the new rain. Two guys sitting in two chairs lookin' at the new rain . . . As a motorcycle rider, you have to be aware of the new rain. The pores of the road clogged with sticky oil open up when they feel the new rain, the baby rain, washing away the old grime, the oil. It doesn't even try to do it, it just happens. If I didn't slip on the first risings and could make it through an unlit night, then surely I could harness the new morning.

I took the suggestions that Bob made regarding old blues and rock 'n' roll records very seriously. My buddy Pretty Tony Mangurian had a little studio in Manhattan at the time, and he and I got together and checked out some of the records Bob wanted me to hear. I was already familiar with these records, but had not heard them in a while. Bob was right. They were vibrant and had a sense of urgency rising up from their sounds. Tony and I played along—we closed our eyes and transported ourselves to the Charlie Patton orchestra, fast and furious. We piled on heaps of renegade overdubs. I squinted until Mangurian's hole-in-the-wall Manhattan studio turned into Link Wray's cabin; people beating on walls, shouting "Fire and brimstone," the ghost of Bo Diddley, maraca dominating the blend, Little Richard lookin' in the window—"Good Golly Miss Molly!" Link's rockabilly, twangy surf-sound guitar, even the banjo had gotten in there, somebody drumming on a suitcase. The complexity of the rhythmic interplay is staggering. Link and his friends had funneled varied musical sources into a paradigm. The Link Wray cabin—a mini Delta in itself. If a drummer only ever had Wray's "Fire and Brimstone" or "In Time" by Sly and the Family Stone from a record called *Fresh* to listen to, they would likely be fine.

Link Wray was half-breed, and for that matter, so was Elvis. James Brown got some of that in him, too. The native blood also runs through my veins, just a small amount, but enough to keep me connected, even if only by some distant genetic instinct. I love those old Link Wray records, and if you listen to "Fire and Brimstone" you will hear that the complexity in the layerings relates (at least rhythmically) to the records I've tried to make, or at least to the record I was wanting to make with Bob. Tony and I listened back to our jams, and selected the best, inspired group of bars—say eight-bar sections. We then deleted the source inspirations and just listened to our performances—they had a vibe. Even in the absence of the sources, there was a vibe. This was good. Tony and I had two or three sessions like this, and I left the Manhattan studio with fifteen or so grooves that might work for *Time Out of Mind*.

At this point, Bob was rolling down to my own studio regularly. This was the one in Oxnard, California, the old Mexican theater known as the Teatro. The place had been abandoned for a long time. My engineer buddy Mark Howard and I found stacks of old Mexican movie posters in the projector booth. They were fantastic, from a time when you had to leave your house for entertainment. The county fair—the cherry pie competition, the raffle, the door prize, people dressed up, somebody making love in the grass—it was all there. Howard and I transformed the popcorn/reception area of the Teatro into the most beautiful display of poster art. I didn't realize their value, and I wish I still had a few of them now. I believe that Bob also has a regard for art of this kind, as is evident in his current adverts when he tours. The Mexican poster display set a nice tone, and I believe Bob had a good time turning up at the Teatro.

It was always just Bob, Howard, and me. Pretty Tony later came in for a stretch of demos, as I wanted him to be around to help out with the technology, especially regarding the loops that we had already built in New York. Bob is a roaring piano player with a great left hand, and he made my old Steinway sound like a barrelhouse full of birds. The vocals he sang at the piano were full-bodied and deep. Tony and I monitored the prepared Manhattan loops in our headphones (as we were the timekeepers) and Bob played and sang along with us. The loop could then be heard in the overall blend for playbacks and mixes. We had stumbled upon a magic formula. We had found the sound for *Time Out of Mind*. I was so excited I couldn't sleep. Bob had written powerful lyrics, and I felt that we were on the verge of something great. We had found a way to embrace the sound of old American records, and my mind started to race. This could be the greatest record ever. Bob was at a lyrical peak, and as for myself, I saw the potential for a new level of sonics on the horizon. I became obsessed with the idea of making a heartfelt, dangerous, and monumental record.

Bob's visits became more frequent. We had no schedule. He turned up like a ghost whenever he wanted. Everything around us was unorthodox. The eeriness of the Teatro was making its way into the work; behind closed doors, time was nonexistent. It could have been any era. We had designed a license to disobey the rules of contemporary technology. The demos were dripping with emotion, but our minds were clear.

Howard had never been to school, but had a wealth of knowledge acquired through years of road experience and by having lived through impossible demands placed upon him by myself. This is a guy who had driven an eighteen-wheeler to Mexico and set up my studio on a mountainside outside Todos Santos, on the coast of Baja. We had been to battle on many challenging projects. His stamina for building studios in unlikely locations could not be surpassed by anyone. We had telepathic communication, but when that needed to be supplemented, Howard would strap a walkie-talkie to his head with a bandanna, and I would direct him from the back of the Teatro by shouting into my walkie-talkie, preparing him for upcoming twists and bends in the arrangements, like a general ordering him to take aim into hillsides. It was a great system that I have never seen anyone else use.

I had pretty much reached a crossroads in my work life. Domestic life had not even come close to taming me and I felt a deep connection to the song "Desperado." I would lock myself in the Teatro and play my steel guitar for weeks at a time, every drop of sorrow in me dripping down to my fingers and onto the steel guitar. It's not a comfortable place to be, but I can safely say that those isolated sessions were part of the emotional building blocks for *Time Out of Mind*. Whatever I was feeling at that time would be part of the album.

Bob paid more visits, and the recordings became greasier and more strange and displaced-sounding. Pretty Tony Mangurian, a tortured soul in his own right, already had displacement living inside him, a bandito drifting, like he had just stepped out of one of my Mexican movie posters. Howard and I were still dedicated to the motorcycle culture. Not only was the Teatro a great shop for recording music, it was a great showcase for the motorcycle collection. Back in the late eighties, we had acquired a masterpiece of a Harley-Davidson for Bob. Motorcycle camaraderie had been our friend then, and was still our friend now. Howard and I had made some good new Harley-Davidson repair contacts in the Oxnard area. When Dylan told us that he was having trouble with his old Harley, we were able to hook him up. With the help of the motorcycle, Bob, Howard, and I were back on even ground.

Bob had come up through the era of large-displacement American engines known as the big-blocks. Size, power, and torque were top priorities—clearly a time when gasoline was affordable. American designers wanted to provide their customers with that special feeling of lots of horsepower under the hood. The 327 Chevy comes to mind. These 327 cubic inches were available in the most common family model provided by Chevrolet, the 1967 Impala. Engines of this time had power, the lines of the car were sexy, and the bench seats were ideal for making out with your girl on a Saturday night. Long before the air bag and the baby seat, pleasure ran in tandem with practicality.

Harley-Davidson was also at the forefront of the large engine, available as a twin cylinder in their motorcycles. The bike we got for Bob boasted the Shovelhead—an engine design that ran through the seventies and was regarded as one of America's sexiest engines, if not the most reliable. This motor technology came up at the same time as rock 'n' roll, and for me, it was all connected to the sounds of the American records that Bob had referenced.

Certain musical values had not evolved well in America. Many of America's best grooves had pretty much been abandoned. Perhaps this is a by-product necessary to a nation that places a high regard on the new. Perhaps, in order to feel comfortable with building something new, America must be seen to have forgotten the past. Strangely enough, America would soon find itself embracing *Buena Vista Social Club*, a film built on the amazing values of the past. Cuba has not abandoned its best grooves—the artists in that great Wim Wenders film might be in their eighties but they will never be seen as antiquated. A year later *O Brother, Where Art Thou?* would make the country curious about the richness of its spiritual and bluegrass past, if only for a season.

Things were going well with Bob, and I was the most excited I had been regarding production in a long time. Then came the crushing phone call; he wanted to leave the Teatro. He explained to me that it had become evident to him that we needed to assemble a band and make the record in Miami. The Miami part of the call has always mystified me, but I couldn't disagree with his suggestion about assembling a band. Bob had put some thought into this, and when he described the power of Jim Dickinson's piano playing to me, I was left speechless. Bob said if we could get Dickinson, we might not even need anyone else in the building. Dickinson had been a force who Bob was clearly curious about. He was from Memphis, and had been around for much of what Bob felt had been a major influence on American rock 'n' roll. I had to trust Bob on this, as I felt shamefully out of the loop, with no knowledge of Dickinson's work.

Tony Garnier, who was already playing bass in Bob's road band, was invited to play on the record. This was a suggestion I liked, as I was aware of Tony's reputation as a rock-solid player with Louisiana values. He could play any style, and it was comforting to me that he had spent a lot of time in the hidden parts of Louisiana, where some of the only remaining American rock 'n' roll exists. To this day, you can go to dance halls on the outskirts of Lafayette and hear that wonderful dance-hall rock, guaranteed to give you a quiver and tempt you into doing the two-step. Texas also has a few hidden pockets of that original rock 'n' roll culture still alive, like the Continental Club in Austin, but I don't know how long they're going to last.

Garnier is a pillar of a man, always there with a big-brotherly embrace and the musical knowledge to back it all up. Bob suggested other players—Cindy Cashdollar; Bucky Baxter, Bob's pedal steel player; Duke Robillard; Robert Britt; and Augie Meyers. I was familiar with Augie's reputation—he had played on many great Tex-Mex recordings and was regarded as a force on the Vox combo organ, pretty much a shuffle player. This was good, as a few of Bob's songs had gone up that street. The shuffle is often referred to as a thing of the past, but it's always in my mind, and it's a hard thing to get right. I knew that if we had Augie, the skank upbeat would be authentic and soulfully played.

Bob and I talked about Miami. Perhaps we could find a theater or banquet hall with a stage, which sounded exciting to me, especially as Howard and I had the gear and the know-how to pull something like this off. Jeff Kramer, Bob's manager, did his best to find us such a location. But in the end it didn't pan out and, as the start date of the record was creeping up on us, we opted for a more conventional studio, which turned out to be Criteria Sound.

Howard and I chose a selection of my favorite equipment from the Teatro. Two small sidecar Neve consoles would act as the preamp stations (for all the microphones to plug into). We had a simple and strict rule—keep the main console constantly in mix-and-listening mode, which would enable us to lay down a mix anytime, even in the middle of a band-track day. Experience has taught me that you never know when you are going to get a mix; leaving ourselves open to every possibility has always been ingrained in my work technique, and so the philosophy continues.

There were other pieces of equipment, like the Sony C-37A microphone that I had used on Bob's voice back in '88, some LA-2A compressors and Sennheiser 409 mics that are great on guitar amps, and many other pieces of processing gear that I won't go into—I don't want to give away all my secrets. The equipment was put in a truck with a couple of motorcycles, and Howard drove it from California to Florida. When I arrived in Miami, Howard had already been there for a few days, and like he always does, he had the room completely set up. There was one problem, though—the room didn't sound any good. The drums sounded crap and the room was dead. The usual studio design clichés were there—lots of angled wood, a few rocks on a wall, carpeted hallways—and you couldn't imagine any fragment of rock 'n' roll existing in there at all. My heart sank and I began to pine for the Teatro. The Teatro had vibe dripping from the walls. Now in Miami, it felt like everything that I had worked for had slipped through my fingers. My amazing turn-of-the-century Steinway grand piano was collecting dust in California as I stared into the mouth of a generic Yamaha monster.

The studio manager could obviously feel my disappointment and suggested that there might be a possibility of us moving into the orchestra room down the hall. The problem was, the orchestra room had already been booked by someone else. After a few days of negotiation, we were allowed to switch rooms. The move cheered me up considerably, as the dimensions of our new digs fit into my way of looking at *Time Out of Mind*. My way of looking at *Time Out of Mind* was about "depth of field." Take old Dr. John records, for example. When you listen to Dr. John records, you can feel and imagine the presence and placement of people in a room; the background singers, for example, sound like they are in the back of the room and they probably were. Given that Bob wanted a large group of people in the band, I treated it as an opportunity to chase my dream of great natural depth of field on a record.

The new room proved to be much better than the initial dead room. There was enough space for our many road cases and we went as far as setting up a little workshop for guitar repairs and wiring up the different kinds of adapters that I always seem to need. Bob had not arrived yet, so I spent time with the band refining our setup. I chose to position Bob at the grand piano over to one side of the studio, with my rig about five feet from him so I could read his facial cues and then conduct the rest of the band accordingly. We rented a pump organ for Dickinson, and Augie had his organ rig behind a sliding-glass door, but he wasn't too far away. The drummer Bob had invited did not work out, and I had to do what I've hardly ever done—send him home and call in some heavyweights.

Brian Blade is a southern drummer, and in my experience southern drummers have always had the best feel for blues, funk, and shuffles, the kinds of grooves we were about to investigate. Blade learned to play in his father's church, and so he had those authentic church grooves down and was used to serving singers. The subtleties of a drummer's strokes are important to me on records. Perhaps live you can get away with a few rough turns in the bend of a song, but there is no forgiveness on a recording, and I was not about to accept a risk in this touchy territory. There have been songs that have changed the way I see drums working on records, like the way Sly and the Family Stone used a drum kit and a rhythm box on "In Time," one of the great marriages of technology and human playing and definitely one of the funkiest tracks ever. And on the Supremes' version of "You Keep Me Hanging On" there are two acoustic drummers. In one speaker you have the more conventional kit, and in the other, a second kit plays a sort of percussion part—it's a great sound.

The twin-drummer idea has always appealed to me and, given that Bob had invited a larger group to play, I rolled the dice and also invited Jim Keltner. Jim is a seasoned, accomplished, and unusual drummer. Brian would be the engine, as he is the master of the sock cymbal (high-hat), and Jim would be the percussionist, the secret passage to unknown surprises. The idea worked; Brian was there with his deep soul, the church in him dripping from every stroke, the sound of a long history of dedication flowing through this young man. Jim had played with Bob before, and beyond his ability to fit in with Mr. Blade, he brought with him a certain kind of wisdom; later in the project he would also be a shoulder for me to cry on when things got tough. The two drummers sat close together and I felt I had made the right decision.

Tony Mangurian had also arrived. I wasn't trying to have these three drummers play all at once; I wanted Tony there as the gatekeeper of the technology we had prepared early on in Manhattan for the project. On "Million Miles" and "Highlands," for example, the grooves that we had built were the mood-setting foundations, essentially dictators of feel. We piped the prepared grooves into the headphones of the drummers, and no matter what happened around the room, they were there as beacons of time and vibe. This technique was particularly helpful in "Highlands." This song is very long, and part of its beauty is that it never budges in tempo, like a long walk under a starlit sky, a constant canopy embracing the ever-evolving story that Bob wanted to tell.

Bob had once told me that you "can't buy feel," and I agree with him. You might be in the best studio with the best people and intentions, and you may not get it on that day; this is all part of the ongoing mystery of the studio. Waiting for the magic is not a comfortable place to be, because it can wear people out and I could not afford days like that, and so the Lanois/Mangurian New York City preparations were my insurance policy. I knew I could trust the feel of these preps, and they could be an instant remedy to a troubled day. After all, this was a Bob Dylan record, and we would have his attention for only so long. Bob moves fast and fresh, and the minutes you have him for could be minutes of genius unfolding. I didn't want to waste them. Other producers had wasted those precious Dylan moments, by not noticing them flying by, those molecular pieces looking for congregation. That was it, we were a congregation—our denomination could not be described, it would disintegrate before anyone knew anything about it. We would already have left Miami by the time anyone would even hear about it. Vaporized outside of memory, like *Time Out of Mind* had never happened. Even the musicians involved would be mystified by the finished work, even on the stage of the Grammys. Even when we were holding the Grammy for Best Album of the Year, Tony Garnier said to me that he couldn't remember how it all had happened.

Technological challenges are fine, as years of experience allowed me to land on my feet at any challenge. But psychological challenges are the slippery ones. Questions like "Why are you doing this?" would come up, and I wasn't doing it for the money. The truth of the matter is that I don't care very much about "record production." I always thought "producer" was a stupid title that I had been given, like I was a dog or something, wearing a collar that says producer, or some tag-wearing, obedient subservient member of a convention, or a disposable and replaceable serviceman at a parts counter. "Let's bring Lanois in and get that Lanois magic sound," as if it's like bringing in a stylist that places a yellow tie on you, and then has you dancing with pretty girls. I am not a stylist. I am a child of God, of my mother, of the values that guide my work. I am a child of dedication and possibilities, of experimental sonics that want to fly over the cuckoo's nest of both postmodernism and tradition. I love the past and respect the forefathers and mothers of significant music, but I want to make groundbreaking futuristic records.

One of the reasons I accepted the invitation to make *Time Out of Mind* with Bob is that I wanted my sonics to be challenged by a level of lyric that only Bob could write. Bob has always seen the studio as a place of documentation. That's why he values the presence of a good band. Who could argue with the idea of documentation? But is every snapshot in the end a portrait? It takes a lot of care and curiosity to see the possibilities in that portrait. I wanted the shadows to hold hidden secrets, for the details to pique the curiosity of a viewer, time and time again. I wanted the sunlight in the portrait to outlive us all, and be blazing with premonition, hope, and redemption, to be the ultimate piece of documentation of '97—the documentation of the dedicated minds of *Time Out of Mind.*

I lived in the Marlin Hotel and rode my bike to work every

day. The Marlin was owned by my old friend Chris Blackwell, who had been a mentor to me all along, even if in a distant manner. Chris had been a sort of godfather to the U2 projects I had been involved with since the eighties. He had been a big part of the export of Jamaican rock 'n' roll. I call it rock 'n' roll because what we know as the most famous reggae music of Jamaica—say Bob Marley—had an interesting evolution, from calypso to rock steady to ska, etc. When I spoke to Chris about it all, he explained to me that the reggae music everybody loved around the world had had its birth in the studio—in fact it had not been a documentation of what was happening on the street. It was people like Lee "Scratch" Perry that had stumbled onto a "sound" using repeat-echo machines and other gadgets that turned up on the recording gear of the time. These early pioneers had invented a sound that would speak to the world and that held the four vital ingredients—sexuality, godliness, joy, and groove. The Lee Perry sound would become the pedestal at which the likes of Bob Marley could stand and let their sermons be heard.

As I listened to Chris, I realized that what he was talking about was more than just the basic process of documentation. It was also the process of invention. The Jamaican studio had been the birthplace of a form. The studio people were artists, not just technicians. If I had been born twenty years earlier, I likely would have been more of a traditional documentary recording person, but that wasn't me. My years with Eno had provided me with an appetite for innovation, and so my time in Miami was all about providing Bob with a futuristic way of looking at his work.

Howard had a full-size Harley and I was riding a BMW GS Enduro. We would leave the studio each night promising to be good boys and not race. As soon as we got to the open stretch across the causeway, the race would begin. Howard was a better rider, but my bike was faster. We knew where the cops had their usual radar spots, and we would wave at them as we rode by at 30 m.p.h., to then start the race back up when they were out of sight. The motorcycle kept me sane. I love the commitment required to handle these dangerous iron beasts. You would not find us rummaging through a bag at a stoplight, never on a cell phone, not reading a script or plucking an eyebrow. We were dedicated men of the Iron Horse. The psychological skill required to read the faces of drivers behind the wheels of cars is a constant benefit to the mind that deals with the psychological challenges of the studio.

Howard and I had reached a level of communication where one wink of an eye or one gesture of a finger was all we needed to know the direction of the ship. It might be mysterious to some why *Time Out of Mind* drips blood, lyrically but also sonically. It's because the forefathers of the art form were all there, at least in my mind: Eno, Lee "Scratch" Perry, even Arthur Alexander and Hendrix. In case anyone is interested, Arthur Alexander is a hero of mine. Check out his high-hat sound on his song "Anna," long before the Beatles came along. Sometimes I think I'm losing my mind, referencing an obscure high-hat part from the fifties, living with the warbling guitar sound of Blind Willie Johnson—ghosts in my head, constantly tugging at my sleeve, and the pop music industry looking at me like a last standing member of a fading veterans' club. I was walking the blues tightrope—how to operate within a form and avoid the roadhouse sand trap to the left and the barroom tar pit to the right.

Bob had his own set of concerns, I'm sure; suddenly a room full of musicians and Lanois running around like a worried hen. My brother Bob had been invited on my recommendation to film the recording process, so he was there too, and perhaps this was not a great idea, as Dylan was not really in a filming frame of mind. My brother was asked to go home and nothing ever happened with the footage he shot. If I remember right, at least half of the Miami session was filmed, but all that footage was handed on to Dylan's camp. The *Time Out of Mind* chapter was still very much a chapter of privacy and mystery for Bob. He went much more public after that album. He wrote *Chronicles* and released a documentary film with Martin Scorsese's help, and then to everyone's surprise, hosted a fantastic satellite radio show called *Theme Time Radio Hour.*

Pool halls, late nights, hangin' out with the wrong crowd suggest a misspent youth. But what about those who operate outside of the usual confines of education? What were people thinking about Bob Dylan as he went on a mysterious teenage lyrical pilgrimage? What goes on in somebody's head cannot be measured by any system. Imagine becoming a master of the pen or a master of the word without anybody pushing you around. The misspent or well-spent youth of Bob Dylan allowed him to reach the level of Ph.D. outside of any guidelines and become a national treasure of lyricism. Every mother should hope that her child reaches such a position of independence. I cherish my time spent with the man himself.

I had pretty much memorized all of Bob's songs, given that I had been through the demo-making process. As I listen to *Time Out of Mind*, I hear my angry Goldtop (my gold-top Les Paul, circa 1956, with a Vox AC30 amplifier, circa 1962) charging through the tapestry of our invited guitar players. I also had my Mando guitar, which turns up on "Standing in the Doorway," playing the hook leading up to Bob's vocal, an innocent heart in the presence of lost love. It plays the role of hope, reminding you of the reasons you got into all this to begin with.

Bob likes strong hooks, as I do, and I can remember he and I both plugged into my Vox amp, playing the riff to "Love Sick" as an overdub. This was a nice reminder of how musical two instruments in one amp can be. It's the same philosophy as sending a few different sources of sound to one summing amplifier, the way I've heard they worked on early Beatles recordings—lots of instruments stacked up on just a few tracks. There is a musical result to be had from a one-point source, two guitar players in one amp or four singers on one mic. As technology has evolved, we've gotten further away from this idea. Contemporary recording devices offer an endless amount of tracks, and so people use them. The components of contemporary records all exist on isolated tracks. But the components of rock 'n' roll records from the fifties existed in a group, because isolated tracks were not available. That limitation in technology forced people to make decisions about blends that they could not change their minds about. Simply put, mixing decisions were made along the way and not just on "mix day." The one-point source is a musical friend. If rock 'n' roll was meant to be spontaneous, perhaps options are the enemy.

I felt a darkness spreading like an ether. Everything I ever fought against was spilling down the walls like blood in a horror movie. Clichés are like scabs, you can only shake 'em off after healing. My past had a lot of scabs. Years of record making back in Canada with studio musicians. What an idea: studio musicians. It was all too close to the jingle-making factories for my taste. We were walking a tightrope. How can you get "soul" out of musicians who have done too much? I had to remind myself of why I had gotten into all of this to begin with, which was probably the same reason that everybody else in the room got into it. We love music.

Cindy Cashdollar is beautiful, and I wanted her to play beautifully. Without direction, musicians can go on autopilot. I wanted the playing to have a sense of purpose—no filler, every note living in harmony with the vocal. When the singer sings, you might do best to play nothing or the sound of nothing, just a breeze, that's okay. Like a Nelson Riddle arrangement: wait for the singer to be finished and then play with harmonious relevance, or just stab the hook, like the "slam slam" of "Love Sick." Rambling responses might have had a moment in Nashville somewhere in the time of bluegrass, at a time when fast-flash guitar picking might have attracted regard, but this was not a tourist attraction. That had all been done before. I was very happy to have the souls of our invited guitar players be simply hanging in the wind, just to be trembling leaves. No Nashville flash pickin', no hee-haw, no straw—just characters in the landscape: shadows, dew on the meadow, rough-cut pine, barbed wire, open fields, or a herringbone motif disappearing into infinity, however Bob's storytelling dictates what you might play. This was an atmosphere. You had to leave your clothes at the door to step into the future.

The large orchestra room accommodated the little workshop that I mentioned earlier, plus a little private area curtained off from the rest of the studio where Bob liked to have his meal. He had a friend with him and they'd have some time to talk in privacy during the eating hour. There was a parking lot right outside the studio-loading door where Bob and I would slip out and discuss our approach to the next song.

When you have a large group in a room, instructions must be Shakespearean. There's no room for too much fat or indecision. Bob took me aside. The parking lot was our "war room." Angles and choices of grooves were private matters. We had two of the best drummers in the world waiting in the orchestra room. I wanted the groove to drive this record. Atmospheres are like mist—beautiful only when viewed against the mountain range, but take away the mountain and you may just drive by and not know the mist. Keltner and Blade—my mountain range. Memories of "Sad-Eyed Lady of the Lowlands," a waltz groove from Bob's past, came to mind, a fertile mountain that might be just the bedrock for Bob's "Standing in the Doorway."

Bob listened. His songs can go so many ways. I've been in the room when there was the sudden surprise of a change in time signature, or suddenly a different key. I never knew if he was doing this to keep the musicians on their toes—after all, we are only cats landing on our feet. The shifting of the time signature, maybe that's good. It might just add a little more punch, and knock the predictability out of a pose. I was playing my little mandolin, and a hook started building in my head

Tradition, tradition, tradition—Bob and I both had plenty of it under our belts. How could this generic parking lot have become my office, with a chain-link fence blocking out the badlands—the same kind of fence that my tongue had stuck on when I gambled and licked it, on the edge of some junkyard by a frozen lake in Canada. But here I didn't want to keep the badlands out. We were in the badlands, and everybody wanted to know what was going on in the bad man's head.

All the waltzes that I had ever known flashed in front of my face like it was my last minute. That was it—the waltz. My Keltner/Blade mountain range. The rest of us were mist and smoke machines, we only needed to provide a little atmosphere so Bob could be "sufferin' like a fool." My little mandolin floated on top, like the old dozen roses. We just needed another three weeks—perhaps the fence was there to keep the animals in, rather than the badlands out. Decision made, Bob and I walked back in and went public. "Standing in the Doorway" was now a waltz.

My mando guitar was overdubbed as soon as we had the track. Bob was very supportive of my little melodic invention, as it qualified as a riff. We had reached a harmonious place, and Howard provided us with the most inspired playbacks. They sounded so great that Howard and I took careful notes of our settings, as they would likely have to be replicated later.

Bob's vocals were penetrating and had that sound that would frighten a young child. Perhaps Neil Young's theory could apply here—if it sounds dangerous, you're on the right track. Howard and I had introduced Bob to a treated vocal sound that inspired him. We sent his vocal back into a little Gretsch guitar amplifier. It was a little tube amp from the sixties, and it seemed to automatically give the vocal that sound of the old records Bob had recommended I listen to. I made sure that this vocal sound was heard on all playbacks, as it is always a good idea to juice people up around the room, and I wanted Bob to know that we had unlocked the secret of those old Charlie Patton records. The little Gretsch amp was my secret weapon to recapturing that overdrive sound. Bob was pleased with the device, and there were times on mixes where the amp sound was as loud as the clean signal straight from the mic. Different bands have come out since using that sound, and in fact it was pretty much the same sound I had used on Bono's vocal in the early nineties on a song called "It's No Secret" on *Achtung Baby.*

Everything was moving along well, and we cranked out the tracks, sometimes two a day. The vibe was good and I could sense that Bob was appreciative of Brian Blade's presence. He was the unlikely inclusion, and we all knew that he had brought in a feeling of truth and dedication. This was not a hired gun, not a man who was jaded by having done too many sessions. He came in with a pure heart, with virtuosity in every stroke, and I felt he had found a friend in Jim Keltner. They made a fine team and I was a proud papa. Bob continued to tear me apart with the lyrics; his constant amendments seemed to improve the songs at every turn. He even wrote a song on the spot called "Make You Feel My Love." Built on top of a classic chord sequence, the vocal is fat with emotional delivery. I was even able to forgive the second-rate piano that I'd been forced to use. Bob was flying high, as I was.

Perhaps this is the right time to explain what a searching person I am. It gets covered up with work. It is a kind of genetic family condition and I really don't know where it comes from—this constant questioning of results and forever imagining improvements. Apparently my father was this way, a sort of wanderer who would not keep friends. He would be impressive in a new situation, and then disappear and lose touch with people. It is built into my character and I don't want to hurt people with it, but I can't help it. There have been many times where this dysfunction has added to the creation of songs that became hits, which include complex emotions woven into their tapestries. It is a constant struggle for me and I don't like to subject others to my searching, but there are moments of epiphany. It's laboratory work, really, and any scientist will tell you that research is trial and error, and sometimes by-products are more interesting than what you thought you were supposed to be going after. Doubt is just part of the recipe. Bob is the opposite—very sure of himself, and pointed in a specific direction. I love that about him.

So there I was in Miami, the kid from a steel town wondering what the hell it was all about, banging into brick walls, hoping to find a way to make it all work. I was not about to be a casualty of mediocrity. Innovation is costly—it eats away at your life, your time. It makes a mockery of you as you stand there with your pants down, as you make noises in the studio. It laughs at every failure and has no patience for dreams. I still suffer the blows of insecurity, as I get it all wrong twenty times, but on the twenty-first time I may get it right, and the gray clouds will let sunshine through.

Mangurian was sent home when things took a dark turn. I had wanted a "hit" for Bob. A "hit" means a great song, a rendition that touches people's hearts in a universal manner. I felt that Bob's song "Can't Wait" held that chance. We had it on the demo—a roaring vocal delivery, Bob at the piano, me on the Les Paul, and Mangurian on the kit. We were now rerecording the song, and I felt that its potential as a hit was disintegrating in front of my eyes. I begged Bob to reconsider the feel of the demo. I even sent Mangurian out there for a take, but Bob didn't have the desire and Tony was sent home. "Can't Wait" has a convincing feel on the record, but it did not become a hit. "Can't Wait" had been my ace, and now my arms had been paralyzed and I couldn't move to play my card.

Bob is a sort of jazzman—he likes to deliver what he feels at the moment, and who can argue with that? But I was asking him to study not only Charlie Patton, but his own demo successes. I wanted to make sure the groove was right. Build and maximize. If I could align myself with some of the hip-hop greats, get your groove first and then build your song. Bob didn't go for it and that was pretty much the end of Miami. I never got him a hit. I got him a Grammy, but not a hit. *Time Out of Mind* will remain a great American classic, but I didn't get him a hit, and I could have.

The Miami sessions came to a close. Howard packed everything up and drove back to California. We would soon huddle up back at the Teatro, where it had all started. Bob had reviewed the recordings, as I had, and there was definitely something there. He started turning up at the Teatro with lyrical amendments and entirely new stanzas that Howard and I worked in, couplets floating from song to song till they found their most potent home. We had to technologically mimic the leakage in Bob's vocal to insure that his insertions were flawlessly made to fit. Bob's wish to change some of the chords, long after the band had gone home, meant that I replayed all the harmonic instruments, punching into Tony's bass track, sitting at the piano, punching in minor chords where there had been majors and so on. I didn't mind all this, it was all part of the same philosophy that had always driven me—feel first, and everything else will follow.

Bob asked if I had a camera, and would I take a photograph of him. I said I would. In fact, I take good pictures even though I wouldn't be regarded as a professional. I shot one roll of 35 mm black and white on my old Nikon military-grade camera. There was little light in the Teatro, and so I held the camera on a guitar case for stability and gave the film a three-second exposure as Bob sat in the middle of the fantastically equipped theater, holding my baby Stella acoustic guitar. The contact sheet came back and Bob chose his favorite of the shots taken. I organized a nice large print to be made as the master, but in the end Bob preferred the vibe of the contact sheet, and that became the record cover.

When Bob went home after his vocal repairs, Howard and I worked on mixes. The Miami mixes sure had a sound, and it took a while for us to get back to that sweaty Florida feel. My console was the same brand as the Miami console, but a different model. They had a Neve 8078 and mine was an 8068, same era and all. The 8078 had four-band equalizers and mine had three bands. The three-band isn't a lesser animal than the four-band; it's just a little different. Probably the biggest difference was that we were in a different place in time.

As I rode my motorcycle to deliver my mixes to Bob, I passed by a strange and renegade community between Ventura and Malibu, in a sort of sand basin that was essentially a relative of the Los Angeles River without the concrete (the Los Angeles River is a giant drain to the sea built to accommodate flash-flood runoff that can happen during the rainy season). This between-Ventura-and-Malibu basin was not covered in concrete, in fact this area was pretty much rural, as money had not come in to rebuild or divert. The basin had been occupied by a community of perhaps illegal migrant workers who pick the strawberries for America. They had seen this unused land as a place to live, and were living under homemade roofs with walls made out of sticks and stones. What they had built was not dirty, they were not dirty, and their thoughts were not dirty. They were simply working hard, building their nests and feeding their children, living like the birds and animals around them. They were honest. They were not placing more demands on the earth, and in a respectful and harmonious way, had settled in the best manner possible.

At this point, having been in Oxnard for a few years running my studio, I had a relationship with some cops in the area. When I was hanging out with one of my police friends, I was told a story that broke my heart. This community would soon be smashed up and the people there driven away.

I arrived at Bob's hotel, where someone greeted me with gentleness but suspicion. They recognized that I was not a president killer, took the tapes, and I rode off into the night. Gradually the record was completed. I have to say that Bob's attention to mixing details at this point was impressive. He would scrutinize the mixes, and report back to the Teatro with razor-sharp observations. He also went on to overdub a few electric guitar parts; in fact, some of the solos are his. The naïve spirit and stabbing bravado of Bob's playing has always appealed to me. The events around this time are a bit of a blur, but I know that Bob got really sick, some peculiar infection around his heart. We talked about it some, and he told me that it had been more pain than he had ever felt.

Months later I saw Bob on the Pacific Coast Highway, wearing a cowboy hat and driving a nice old El Dorado. We pulled over, had a coffee, and talked about life. I've not seen him since, but I believe I got a Christmas card from him once. I felt relieved when the ultimate conclusion to our work turned up on television. "Love Sick" had become the theme for the new Victoria's Secret sexy women's underwear campaign. The penetrating sound of my Goldtop Les Paul and Bob's Telecaster had reached the masses. I felt it had all been worthwhile—Bob and I had had our hit.

Bob has gone on to make records since *Time Out of Mind* in my absence, and from the bottom of my heart, I wish him the best and I feel our lives crossed for reasons beyond our practical understanding. I think we could safely say that both Bob and I are eccentric people. Our eccentricities may be running in two different directions, but they are definitely running.

Bob called me in the middle of the night . . .
I said, "Bob, what time is it?"
He said, "It's dark out"
I said, "Where are you?"
He said, "I'm drifting."

15

THE WALKING MULTITRACK

Eno and I wandered through the corridors of the medina in Fez, Morocco, wearing digital Minidisc recorders around our necks. The medina is the ancient part of Fez, essentially a marketplace. Nonstop cacophony, people pulling and pushing every which way, with an incredible range of merchant action. The small alleyways cannot accommodate cars, only donkeys, people, and pushcarts. Every few feet presents a wildly different display, goat heads at one boutique, carpets and woodcarvings at the next. Some of the lanes are frighteningly narrow. Apparently, part of the defense mechanism of the city involved luring an enemy into the medina, with the understanding that they'd simply get lost and not be able to find their way out of the labyrinth; a sort of ancient roach motel.

Eno and I had coincidentally purchased the same model of Sony digital recorder, equipped with stereo microphone and speakers, and as an experiment we recorded our walk through the medina. Sometimes we were close together talking, other times we were separated by the market action, say twenty feet apart, and then we would wander back together. After our twenty-minute outing, we returned to the hotel to listen to our recordings. We placed our machines on the table and put both of them into playback mode. After a couple of tries, we had them synchronized, and the playback was fantastic. The result was a true representation of the depth of field we had experienced on our walk. It got me thinking about the walking multitrack system.

Armed with half a dozen of these little recorders in my jacket, I could turn up anywhere and strategically place them, set to record, in a room, say, where there was musical action. Because the recorders run on batteries, this could be done without making too much of a fuss; no extension cords, no cables, no crew. After the event, the content from my little recorders could be dropped into my main computer, much the same way that snapshots from a digital camera can be dropped into a laptop for editing and sequencing. My renegade recordings can now be easily synchronized by shifting them around a bit (an option readily available in all laptop sound recorders) and, voila! A multitrack recording with the curious advantage of a six-point stereo source, relative to where the pocket recorders were initially placed. These little machines cost about $300 each.

In a similar way, on reviewing footage of session documentation, I've noticed that the sound from the video camera's onboard stereo microphone is always exciting, as it shifts relative to the camera movement. What an exciting dimension to consider, microphones moving relative to the action in the room. This could be the future of the next dimension of depth of field in audio recording. I could walk onto any plane, my six little recorders and a notebook in my trench coat, and be ready to record anything anywhere. I think I may have finally found a good use for digital technology.

Flashback to Eno, 1980. The introduction of the Walkman was the beginning of the "on the go" personal entertainment station. I can remember a dinner-table Eno rant. The Walkman promised mobility, but introduced isolation. Yes, it's wonderful to be an individual. Well-jogged, fit, and fabulously self-sufficient, but the earplugs put out a message: "Don't bother me now." What might be regarded as an antiharassment tactic could also be viewed as the erosion of neighborhood "good morning" etiquette. Twenty-five years later, every face is buried in a computer, every ear is plugged with headphones, the art of proposing a toast has fallen into decline—if you're not writing up a business proposal, you must not be with it. But looking somebody in the eye with cheerfulness and optimism should never fall out of fashion.

TAG-TEAM MIXING

The problem with mixing is that it takes too long. Given that it's usually the last stage in the record-making process, all of the pressure and expectations are coming to a head. Consequently, everybody is piled in a room together, throwing in their suggestions, and it can go on for hours with seemingly no significant changes, just turning up one little high-hat there, turning down one little background vocal somewhere else, and to make matters worse, the computer mixing system has finally kicked the last bit of wind out of any spontaneity.

The remedy: throw everybody out of the room and let one guy do a mix; but he gets only fifteen minutes. This is something Eno and I started a long time ago. I do my fifteen-minute mix, commit it to stereo; Eno then walks in and does his fifteen-minute mix. There's only one rule—you have to lay down a mix after fifteen minutes. Nothing's sacred; you can change anything you want. The back-and-forth tag-team work goes on for, say, two hours. At the end of two hours, you have eight mixes. Every mix will have something unique about it, because each has freshness and spontaneity in its spine.

The two hours have now produced interesting and surprising results. This is good, because it's only a matter of time before the recording studio starts breeding "studioitis," where work just inches along or hardly moves at all. Listening to the playback of these mixes is now fun for the rest of the gang. The time invested in these mixes is small, therefore emotional attachment is not a problem. Even if you have to go back in to have another try, at least this time you already have surprising mixes that can act as a template for a cool blend. Moving fast can make up for a lot of hard labor.

THE BACKWARD TECHNIQUE

Once a mix is done, don't change anything on the console. The effects chain—individual fader levels and idiosyncratic tonal preferences relating to one specific song—will not likely make any sense when you then put up the multitrack for the next song.

Here is the idea: you pour yourself a cup of coffee, sit in the back of the control room, and listen to the songs of your entire album through the complex setup that exists on the console, relating to the song you just mixed.

Result: whacked-out balances, detailed, faraway information is now in the front, meat-and-potatoes information further back, some overdub that was not even meant to be there is now super-loud, the hand-clap part has a crazy echo on it, etc.

Yes, most of it will be laughable, but some of it will not. Some of it will be surprisingly ingenious. For the price of sitting back and having a cup of coffee, you may stumble onto a balance that could be special to the record. Given that objectivity is harder and harder to come by the deeper you get into the process, this simple and fun technique might just put a second wind back into you.

A suggestion: play all the songs on the record twice: once forward, once backward. Backward may very well create fantastic new melodies.

Another nice simple technique I've been using for years: if I stumble onto an effect that I like, I always print it back to the multitrack. Effects are slippery, they can never be dialed up exactly the same on another day. Like the Jamaican reggae recordings, committing to an echo on the original day is better than applying it as an afterthought on a later day.

DON'T ASK ONE BOX TO DO TOO MUCH

After years of frustration regarding communication in the studio, I finally figured it out. My Teatro shop in California was a massive place. I liked listening in the back of the shop while Howard was mixing in the front. By not having my face right in a speaker, I was holding the position of an objective listener, and it was easier for me to have an accurate idea of blend and balance. The problem was, anytime I wanted to make a suggestion to Howard, I had to wave my arms and yell.

Solution: I strapped a headband onto Howard with a walkie-talkie built into it. I could now talk to him from the back of the room with the other walkie-talkie in my hand, kind of like those newscasters who wear little earplugs to receive coaching from the production room. The system was great; I could walk Howard through the twists and turns of an arrangement, I was able to give him countdowns to upcoming background-vocal cues, I could spontaneously call out a spin-echo command, conduct him gracefully on a fade. What a dream come true—communication without a bunch of shouting.

Conclusion: never use a talkback system built into a console, always use a separate talking system.

ROPE ON A LEG

When Eno came to visit me in New Orleans to help with the Neville Brothers' *Yellow Moon* album, we developed the "rope on a leg" communication system. Malcolm Burn, who was engineering, had a habit of always looking down at the console. After failing to get his attention a good few times, Eno, who was about twenty feet from Malcolm, decided that the best way to get his attention was to pull on a rope tied to his leg.

PETER GABRIEL'S COW BARN

Peter Gabriel had not fully finished the lyrics to the songs on *So*. The studio was made up of two rooms: the control room that I hung out in, and the cow barn part, with a big industrial sliding door, where Peter wrote his lyrics. Peter and I had an arrangement: I would fiddle with the sounds in the control room, and he would write his lyrics behind the sliding door in the barn—and then it started, telephone interruptions. Peter would go missing out of the barn and I'd find him distracted on the phone.

Solution: the next time Peter went into the barn, I took these giant railway spikes and nailed him in. The big sliding door was permanently closed. I'm not sure that all the lyrics came out of that one session, but it was a good tone-setter for discipline, even if it almost got me deported from the West Country of England.

MUSCLE MEMORY

The way that a song's components interact and influence the direction of a song is something that I'm still trying to understand, but I know for sure that it happens. As I'm playing a song back through the console, the moves that I make, or volume shifts in the first part of the song, will dictate or inspire the volume shifts for the next part of the song. You can think of it like conversation in a room: sixteen people, someone says something, someone else laughs, the laughter is contagious, and the mood rises to a place of humor. The humor is now the governor of the next bend the conversation will take.

That's how it works with mixing. The blend of the verse builds expectation, therefore the chorus coming around the corner must deliver the punch line that the verse has set up. We've all seen it in a great comic, the joke that gets funnier and funnier. They milk the situation for all it's worth, relative to the response of the room. Or in the proposal of a toast that includes the characters of a room: include your characters, and the moment is more special. That's the way I feel about my ingredients. They are characters in a room, or characters in a play. The words for the play are written and carefully carved in stone, but the delivery of them is up to the actors. The delivery of my ingredients at the console at the moment has everything to do with me, therefore I must know what they look like, know their names, and know where they are. Every character has its own personality, therefore give them each a look that celebrates their uniqueness.

A little voice came to me and said: Think about your ergonomics, think of your brain as a muscle. Let it learn to the point of forgetting, like riding a bicycle. When you move from one idea to another, the brain will operate on its own without having to struggle to recall the first idea. This makes it easier to be a futurist.

Remember when you were in school, and the teacher posted an angel on your homework, or a gold star, or a purple lightning bolt? These little postings in the margins of your work not only built your confidence, but allowed you to connect good content to a symbol. The Rolling Stones have a tongue, and so Danny should have a symbol, too.

Colors for the eye, or little symbols of personality . . . like giving different names to your different children. Not every child has the same name or the same nose. Not every overdub on a multitrack recorder is the same; therefore a visual display of content should turn up on the console as an ergonomic friend. Not one font for all.

Have a look at this diagram:

It shows where the ingredients live, without the blur of a similar font. We've all experienced it. The problem becomes obvious when we purchase and try to use contemporary goods with plastic casings; for example, a nice little recorder that I just bought has a dozen or so adjustment points, with their labeling embossed on the plastic casing. At first glance, I could not differentiate one adjustment point from another. It meant that I had to scrutinize the tiny print on the gray plastic to know what the functions actually were. This makes for a long learning curve. All adjustment points having the same visual personality is not good for eye-to-hand communication. But putting a little dab of nail polish (say, red polish) on the volume adjustment point will quickly train my eye to understand that "red" means input volume. Gold nail polish on the output volume control for my headphones will teach my brain to know that "gold" means headphone volume, and definitely not microphone volume. They are different, and their difference should not be diluted by making everything gray plastic. The cost cutting of mass production should not undermine one's skill or interfere with one's ability to act quickly at the moment of inspiration. A unique color or a little picture speeds up the process of learning your ingredients' locations. Once your brain knows where your ingredients live, you get to be fast, increasing your chances of tapping into the wonderful world of spontaneity.

On a more technical level, my interest in increasing room communication started in the mid-eighties, when I first worked with Peter Gabriel. A manufacturer by the name of Solid State Logic had provided Peter with a fantastic battleship of a console, with a total recall automation system that boasted an onboard computer screen. The screen was a display of:

1. Song arrangement
2. Track listing
3. Clock time of song
4. Fader movement
5. Memory time left for storage

All of these various bits of information were valuable, but could only be viewed one at a time. The display screen was a bit small and lay flat, recessed in the console in front of the engineer. If I wasn't at the engineer's position, I couldn't see the screen, and for that matter, neither could anyone else in the room. And if only one man sees and works at the screen, you have elitism. Elitism leads to isolation, isolation leads to alienation, alienation leads to the breakdown of communication.

Imagine an airplane cockpit with only one tiny screen—it would be madness.

Under what circumstance would it make any sense for your pilot to be allowed to see only one piece of information at a time, that is, only the fuel gauge, or only the altitude, or only engine temperature? The airplane cockpit displays all information, visible to the pilot and copilot. This is a sensible, safe, and fast ergonomic, machine-to-human communication system. My suggestion to Solid State Logic was to solve their problem by having eight small screens on top of the meter bridge, giving everyone access to all the information all the time. I want my control room to be a cockpit, with no hidden information, and so I came up with the idea of a public information system to include all members of the work team, be they engineers, producers, assistants, arrangers, tea boys, guitar techs, musicians, or singers.

Let's start with a public clock, for example. My control room has a clock high up on the wall that displays minutes and seconds relative to the song we're listening to. If the drummer hears a slippery bar, he looks at the clock and knows exactly where a problem lives and can reference that number to talk about the repair with the rest of the team. As simple as this idea may seem, it makes the work go faster, builds momentum, and reduces frustration.

Remember science class in school, the teacher pointing with a stick so that the people in the back row could understand the lesson? My control room has science teacher blackboards. One blackboard with song titles (essentially a menu display of the album) with little boxes next to the titles, reminding us of the chores left to do to bring the song home. Another blackboard is more of a calendar laying out the work schedule and various people's availabilities, and so on, reminders of birthdays, dental appointments, management and record company visits, someone has to fly to New York, the stylists are stopping in, does anyone need a haircut? Zithromax, sleeping pills, painkillers . . . all available Friday at 4:00 from the rock 'n' roll doctor. The PTA meeting, the blood-works report. Everybody out on Thursday night . . . blow out the cobwebs. The bigger the band, the bigger the meeting-to-work ratio, and so the big blackboards are a necessary friend.

16

JAMAICA

The old neighborhoods of Kingston felt dangerous to me. But I had a good driver: Jimmy Cliff. In the presence of royalty, every back alley and every door had welcome in them. I hit it off with Jimmy right away—he was a spirit man, and I felt it. I gave him a little book of Native American proverbs. The wise sayings of many chiefs resonated with him. Our bible was called "That Little Indian Book."

"I Walk with Love" was the first song that Jimmy and I had a go at. The bones of this recording had already been laid, and Jimmy's vocal was killing. I was brought in to spin some kind of sheen around him. I innocently suggested a maraca overdub. This was my attempt to ease into the hand-played feel that I thought the track needed. Jimmy volunteered. Having come up in the Jamaican calypso era, he was no stranger to the maraca. I couldn't believe my ears and eyes as Jimmy shredded through the track with frighteningly skilled hands. I overdubbed an electric mandolin, someone else overdubbed a DX100 electro bass line. The drummer arrived—his high-hat feel just about did me in. Jimmy sang harmony, and then our time was up. I took a mix and walked through a ganja-smoke-filled waiting room, up to Strawberry Hill. I went to bed and woke up in the night.

Perhaps I had come close to death, decades of images crammed into one dream. Helicopter blades whipping over the Blue Mountains, pathways weaving through shantytowns, Kingston on the horizon, my first day at work at Tuff Gong Studios in Jamaica. Tuff Gong, originally a BBC orchestral-style recording studio, had seen a lot of change. Why should a white kid from Canada be able to help Jimmy Cliff? But Chris Blackwell had rolled the dice on me, and brought me into his world in Jamaica.

Blackwell, two generations ahead of me, was pretty much singlehandedly responsible for the export of Jamaican rock 'n' roll (ska, rock steady, reggae). Running in tandem with the explosion of rock 'n' roll, he started his business by bringing Jamaican recordings to Britain in 1959, where the expanding Jamaican population presented a window of opportunity. His first hit was Millie Small singing the song "My Boy Lollipop." It became a smash hit in England, not only in the Jamaican neighborhoods, but everywhere else. This was the beginning of the new Blackwell empire called Island Records. Chris had an ear for what people wanted. Cat Stevens would soon be on his label; Jimmy Cliff and Bob Marley also joined Island and became universal household names. Blackwell remains a cultural monument to originality and risk taking. "Build your audience, and let the campaign follow," was Chris's conclusive statement during a recent conversation.

There was a party booming down the road, with a roadside PA, faces coming up at you, seemingly from a fog. The place was underlit. It had mystery, darkness, and joy, all blended together. Nobody here could afford any lights, but the event seemed to be fine with just a couple of lightbulbs. Underlighting can be dramatic, like a Tom Waits show, lit by the open door of a refrigerator. Renegade roadside action is common in Jamaica. It doesn't take much to get a party going—music, people, food, drink. This sort of congregation, driven by celebration, not restricted by permit application, has a freedom within it: organizing something like this in Toronto would push you into a labyrinth of permit and bylaw complexities. Sometimes freedom is easier to come by in a third-world setting.

The next morning I listened to the track on my blaster system, and it had soul. Soul at the end of one day means you get to go in for a second day. Chris Blackwell trusted that I cared; even though he didn't fully understand whatever it was that I operated by, he knew that Jimmy Cliff was at least in the hands of a committed artisan.

Blackwell likes soul music, and so do I. That's what he likes about the U2 records that I produced with Eno. You can frame your work with whatever you want, but the center must have soul. Blackwell and I have a history; in fact, Island Records has released most of the U2 records that I've worked on. A visit from Chris to the U2 studio prior to the release of an album always gave us the sensation of reassurance from a godfather. I can remember Chris whispering in my ear after listening to "You're So Cruel" on *Achtung Baby*. He said to me, "That's the kind of groove that I like."

On the other hand, the sonic experiments that Eno, U2, and I had brought to the campaign table made for a very full meal for Chris Blackwell to digest. New faces are always hard to pinpoint. Just when you think you've seen it all, in walks that blue-eyed kid with the oyster-pearl complexion, to reduce it all to ashes with a new birth of idealism. One naïve curly haired entrance could knock the dust off of the old guard. Isn't it great when a hit record causes everybody to perk up and look at the same old world in a fresh way? Innovation has always been at the forefront of my priorities, and I was hoping that this simple Canadian appetite was enough to allow me to sit at the table of Jimmy Cliff. Four notes of Jimmy singing the opening of "Many Rivers to Cross" had brought me to tears. It was one hell of a party invitation, but an even bigger hell of a responsibility to take it all to the next level. I'd felt this feeling before, of being thrown to the lions with a sword made of what? Or with no sword at all. Determination was my only weapon.

Flash forward to 2008 and I'm in my Jamaican cottage, recharging the battery after an Eno/U2 marathon in Europe. I'm feeling that old feeling of a new level of confidence that I've only ever felt from breaking new sonic ground. The sketches for the new U2 record are dripping in atmosphere, a different atmosphere than I've ever known before. One of my favorite songs, provisionally titled "No Line on the Horizon," has come to the forefront. Rock songs are always the hardest to come by or at least the hardest to succeed at—the kind of song that will satisfy a hungry crowd in a full-size arena. "No Line on the Horizon" may very well have it: speed, euphoria, and a welcoming animal quality.

"Welcome" is a big part of this U2 record. Open the door and let the listener into the huddle. Believe in what you're doing and they will believe in you. This song is made up of two Larry Mullen drumbeats—one loop, one played—trance-bass relentless; the Edge conducts the chord changes, with me and Eno floating on top, and a nice spitting lyric from Bono, with a catchy yodel, a slight Germanic flavor, a distant relative to "Beautiful Day." My head is still swimming from the delivery of a full lyric by the man himself, while the Edge sang his harmony. This is the kind of rock song I want to listen to.

What a wonderful first day. Day two is not as good. I am depressed after a day of struggle. I concluded that a full day of effort had not brought any improvement to our original Moroccan demo. The cottage I'm in is beautiful, the pounding sea is calming, but I am depressed. I've always taken failure personally and day two was no exception. Doubt had followed me home, and everything became a question. Thoughts of isolation entered my head, images of Canada, snowfall, clean water on the bank of Lake St. Clair, a cabin structurally sound against the elements, my supplies plentiful in the event of a long winter. I'm rethinking everything, my psychological needs, my body's needs. Are we jazz artists, who play something once, never to be repeated again? Why could we not repeat the feel from Morocco? The song had fallen through my fingers like sand. Maybe we were just too tired. The feeling of a bad day in the studio is enough to make me want to become a fisherman.

As I look out over the Caribbean, I see Ramsey coming in in his small boat. Ramsey has lived on the Goldeneye property since Ian Fleming's time, and he goes out every morning to lift his traps out of the sea: he might catch a crab, he might catch a fish. I wave and shout at Ramsey, "What did you catch?" Not enough to eat, he says. There was a time when Ramsey and his fishermen friends could catch enough fish for their own eating, and also for the making of profit. The fish are not so plentiful anymore, they have been depleted, much like the cod off the coasts of Newfoundland. The greed and shortsightedness that allowed massive factory trawler fishing off the east coast of Canada was rumbling in other parts of the world. If every 7-Eleven provides a tuna sandwich, what is happening to the tuna population?

Ramsey comes up to shore, and I ask him if he has any fresh eggs for me; Ramsey's house is right by the chicken house. Ramsey responds that all the eggs have turned into chickens and he is sad to say that the only eggs being served on the property are "electric chicken eggs."

A telephone conversation with Bono about dreams, about hymns of the future, had already set the tone in my head about where we could go. Bono expressed interest in Morocco, which he saw as a crossroads for a new spiritual music that we could tap into. I had never been to Morocco, but already its exotic tones started coming into my head. This is where it gets abstract. As momentum starts to build toward an idea or a dream place, the imagination starts building an image that is real, even if only in a dream state.

The power to dream has always been my friend. Coming up as a kid in Canada, there were times when dreaming was all I had to go on. There was no one around to teach me what I know, and so I would invent something for myself, or go to the radio. The radio broadcasts through my teenage years were fantastic. Hamilton, where I lived as a teenager, is sandwiched between Detroit and Buffalo. At that time these were two of the great soul music cities of America. I got to hear all the greats from the basement of my mother's house. Toronto radio was also innovative. There were a few whacked-out, late-night disk jockeys, probably high on something, who would take their listeners on musical journeys. These guys would play an entire side of an album, and then go into a poetic rant. Radio was my university. None of it seemed to be driven by demographics. Programming belonged to disk jockeys, and not to advertising companies.

This was all happening before music television. I seldom saw guitar-playing fingers on camera; I had to imagine how parts were played. Just about everything around me was made up of dreams. The Sears catalog's display of musical instruments was enough incentive to keep me delivering my morning paper. After enough saving, I could order an electric guitar from Sears, a dream come true. There was only ever one little picture to look at, but that one little Sears catalog picture was enough to go on for months.

Anything else surrounding the picture of this guitar had to be filled in by imagination. I pretty much jockeyed between the two relevant sections of the catalog: the electric guitar section and the girls' underwear section.

When there is not much to work with, the imagination goes wild. The dreaming begins, and in my case the dream magically became reality. I dreamed that I could play "House of the Rising Sun," and then I could. I taught the saxophone player down the street how to play the melody. The rooftop of my mother's house became a rehearsal space. My little band became a window to any music I wanted to play. From the Sears catalog to my mother's rooftop to "House of the Rising Sun" to being at one with my band mate . . . the dream was building. I kept dreaming and building, always adding to an existing formula, never throwing anything away. I kept my dreams in one place, like a little treasure box in my head; stacking them up, like my own books in my own school. Soon the dreams were stacked so high, I felt I could make a contribution to any musical situation. I was seventeen.

For the longest time, my recordings never had good bass. I dreamed about good bass but I wasn't getting it. It always seemed to be on other people's records, and not mine. The ghosts of good bass—Bob Marley, Charles Wright, George Porter of the Meters, James Jamerson—visited me every night. I didn't have any bass players to teach me in my Canadian neighborhood, and so I looked to these ghosts as my beacons and bodyguards. Simply by dreaming about bass and wanting it in my own work, my bass got better. Perhaps through osmosis, my education broadened. Just being near a speaker cabinet for five minutes in a little reggae record store brought me closer to living my dream. My bass education has always been like that, small amounts of strong doses, usually in unexpected dark nightclubs. I recently found myself running out of a nightclub after hearing a cool bass part that I wanted to remember, the way that I've run out of a museum after seeing a Rothko that I liked. That one Rothko will be with me forever, but if I had seen a Picasso, Monet, or Van Gogh at the same point, my image of the Rothko would have been diluted. When I hear a bass line that I love, I run and hide and remember. My collection of dreams built momentum, before I had even been to Morocco, and Eno, U2, and I did create exotic futuristic hymns, just like Bono and I had imagined in our phone conversation.

I felt that we had crossed into new territory, not only with the future hymns idea, but with the Edge's new approach to the guitar. The Edge and I were very excited with the tonal personality of this rising new guitar sound. His tone historically has had a very shining silver sound; this new tone was from deeper in the throat, related to an old-school "Pop Staples" sound (Pop Staples is a great reference point for a soulful, dark, tremolo guitar sound). This new tone seemed kind to the slide. The guttural sound in the low mid-range provided the Edge a new color to run with. I've seen this before, the Edge excited about a sound that leads to the invention of a riff or melody. We in the U2 camp wait for these moments, as they are potentially pillars of sonic identity.

There is a term, "coming into one's voice," that is used to describe finding your own voice as a musician. The finding can happen more than once. I've seen it happen to people I've worked with over the years, as their taste evolves and as life challenges them. It's a sort of seven-year itch. Guidelines that one operates with for the first seven years may not apply to the next seven. The straight-to-the-bone, carved-in-stone, fixed-melody Edge that I had known was stepping into a world of improv. On this last stretch of work in France, I felt that the Edge had a new aura of freedom about him.

The insects and tree frogs created the most beautiful symphony for the firefly light show in my Jamaican cottage. Chris Blackwell was arriving later that night, and I'd been invited to join him for a midnight rum punch. Midnight rolled. I felt like Martin Sheen, standing in front of Marlon Brando at the end of *Apocalypse Now*, Blackwell dimly lit, weaving his hands in and out of his face as he described to me his dream of Oracabessa.

Oracabessa is a town that butts up against the old Ian Fleming estate, on the north coast of Jamaica, not far from Port Antonio. This is where Fleming wrote many of the James Bond novels. Chris bought the estate sometime back and has preserved it ever since. The estate is pretty much as Fleming would remember it, except that six cottages have been added; I use one of them for myself. Oracabessa is a town that has not been touched by development. Blackwell's dream is to turn Oracabessa into the model town of the future. As I flew along the coast of Jamaica, I saw what Blackwell was talking about. Careless quick-profit development was making the Jamaican coastline generic, catering to tourism in volume. Chris wanted Oracabessa to be different: quality construction, futuristic eco-architecture, a town that could not be severed by greed. Oracabessa should blossom with its own individuality. It should not be the home to Burger King. An island that boasts the finest tropical produce and access to fresh fish should be the supplier of the finest foods for Oracabessa. I didn't fully understand Chris, but I've never fully understood a dreamer's campaign. The most idealistic thinkers in my experience have been the most abstract. Blackwell wavered from complexity to simplicity and back to complexity with his description of this ideal town. The residents should be the owners. A balance of commerce, support system for old folks, babies, everyone in between. No politician in Oracabessa could ever grow to be crooked.

Blackwell's delivery was obscure, but it had fire. I had felt a similar sensation years back at a Dublin dinner table, when Bono proposed his idea of debt cancellation—a variation on the idea of jubilee. *Jubilee* is another word for a new start, every fifty years all debts are canceled, and we all start from scratch again. There was debate at the table, as some of the other heads thought it ridiculous to imagine that any banker could agree to not be paid back. Not long after, Bono made debt cancellation a reality.

I could have argued with Blackwell—it's so easy to drop a rain cloud on idealism—but it's best to let ideas be brought to conclusion. Somebody always knows something I don't know. If I had said no in the recording studio to ideas I did not fully understand, I wouldn't have made records with nearly as much soul. Letting something you don't understand come to fruition is an intelligence in itself.

The man who singlehandedly exported Bob Marley's music to the rest of the world was pouring himself into the dream of Oracabessa. I listened and I believed, even if I didn't fully understand. I walked back to my cottage, swimming in these Blackwell ideas. I felt all charged up and brave to pursue my own idealisms. My conversations with him every now and again are a nice reassurance that I'm not going crazy. My idealistic rants always make sense on a night of Chris Blackwell. Downtown Los Angeles, for example, has a wonderful new monument—the Walt Disney Concert Hall, designed by Frank Gehry. I've been thinking about Frank, he is a fellow Canadian. I'm sure he would have an opinion about the condition of the Great Lakes in Canada. I used to swim in Lake Ontario as a kid, but that was pretty much the last chapter of it. Lake Ontario is so badly polluted by human and factory waste that you can't swim in there anymore. If I could be allowed my moment of dream and idealism, how fantastic would it be for me to be able to swim in Lake Ontario again before my time is up?

Idea: In-house waste management—the Space Age return of the septic tank. No toilet in Toronto flushes to the lake. Every building in Toronto manages its own waste. In-house sewage and water treatment, plus in-house collected rainwater. The return of the rain barrel. (The rainy season dumps billions of gallons of water into the sewers. Six months later, people have no water for irrigation because of drought.)

Idea #2: There is a park in Toronto that is very large and not pretty. The grass is yellow and there aren't many trees. The taxpayer's dollar is pretty much maxed out in Toronto, and so there is no cash to fix up the park. Let's call Frank Gehry. Let's ask Frank to rim the park with five hundred Frank Gehry futuristic award-winning villas to be sold to the rich. Each villa sells for five million dollars. Five hundred times five million, and voila! A 2.5-billion-dollar budget provided by the rich, to finance the most futuristic eco-friendly park town in the world. The rich occupy the edge of the park, and they get what they want: a two-hundred-acre backyard, security, privacy, a blue chip investment. The people of Toronto now have access to the best park in the world, complete with exotic botanical gardens, day care for young and old, windmills to generate electricity, year-round swimming, a high-tech information-center library, the best foods, a 24/7 farmers' market, and a considerate, exclusive park police force.

I'm saying all this because change is slow, and these kinds of examples can set the tone for more change to happen. Oracabessa and the Frank Gehry Park are dreams—but that's how everything starts.

I finished my work with Jimmy Cliff. I worked on four tracks with him and left the rest of the business to the Chris Blackwell camp. As I flew over the Jamaican coastline, part of me was concerned about the destiny and direction of Jamaican music. The collective force that existed at the peak of the freedom movement seemed now to be a mirage of sorts, or dust in the distance. The beginning of a new wave of electronically driven dance hall with aggressive rap toppings was coming in, more muscle than soul. It all concerned me, and I wished I'd been born twenty years earlier—I could have been in New York for the Beat Generation, made records with Jimi Hendrix, and been in Jamaica for "Stand Up for Your Rights."

17

FOUR DAYS WITH WILLIE NELSON

Images of the River Liffey in Dublin in 1984, and walking home every night along its banks, the river almost spilling its black ink water into the dockland warehouse area. My home was the Gresham Hotel. I was working with U2 on *The Unforgettable Fire.* My route home would take me by the two Guinness ships, often docked by the studio, having their bellies filled, readying for the twice-a-week Guinness transport to Liverpool. The black calmness of the river at night made it look like a mirror. On a moonlit night I could see my reflection, and when I listened the river spoke to me.

> Oh deep water, black and cold like the night, I stand with arms wide open.
> I've run a twisted line, I'm a stranger in the eyes of the Maker.
> I could not see for the fog in my eyes,
> I could not feel for the fear in my life,
> from across the great divide,
> in the distance I saw a light,
> Jean Baptiste walking to me with the Maker.

My body is bent and broken by long and dangerous sleep,
I can't work the fields of Abraham and turn my head away,
I'm not a stranger in the hands of the Maker.
Brother John, have you seen the homeless daughter standing there with broken wings?
I have seen the flaming sword there, over there east of Eden, burning in the eyes of the Maker.
Oh river rise from your sleep, river rise from your sleep, rise from your sleep.

The lyrics to "The Maker" had come up from the river. The music came out of New Orleans. Now, fifteen years later, a Willie Nelson rendition was about to make this personal spiritual song more public.

Somehow or other, the plan was for me to meet Willie Nelson in Las Vegas, where he was finishing up a performance. The idea was to ride back to California on Willie's bus, where we'd work up the songs for the up-and-coming *Teatro*. Emmylou Harris kindly agreed to jump on the bus with the view of singing the background vocals for this new endeavor.

There is something Spanish in Willie's guitar playing that I love. A European tone, with a Django Reinhardt spark to it. Django, one of the great Gypsy jazz guitarists of Europe, had been an influence on many guitar players, including Willie Nelson. I was looking for an angle for this record that would be fun, soulful, and fresh. As usual, I studied the ingredients that were available to me. The Spanish tone in Willie's playing is what I decided to feature and run with. The motley crew of musicians that I had selected as his band, gypsy enough in themselves, were already waiting for me in the Teatro back in Oxnard. (Just to clarify, my studio in California was called El Teatro because that's what it said on the marquee. Willie Nelson and the gang liked the name, which simply means "theater" in Spanish, and so we decided to use it for his album's title.)

As our song arrangements evolved on Willie's bus, I kept a hotline open with Howard, who was readying the setup at the Teatro. The Teatro was already an advantage to Willie Nelson; it had a dance-hall feeling to it, and the early days of Willie Nelson were all about the dance hall. His early band, in fact, had been a dance band, providing a two-step opportunity for folks wanting a good time on their Saturday night.

Willie's dance-hall repertoire from back in the day included a crowd-pleaser titled "Lonely Nights." He told me that he had been singing the song regularly since those days. I was fascinated with this dance-hall image. The two drummers I had chosen, Victor Endrizzo and Tony Mangurian, could surely put the dance-hall spark into this new and exciting Spanish-Cuban Willie Nelson record.

My instructions to Howard were clear—put Willie Nelson up on a riser, with Emmylou Harris to his left and Danny Lanois to his right. Our two Cuban drummers (as we called them) were set up at one large drum kit—possible because Mangurian plays as a lefty and Endrizzo plays right-handed—with a nice lamppost light overhead and a massive antique ashtray dead center to handle the chain-smoking habits of our *two* drummers. Willie's sister Bobbie sat at a rig that I prepared for her. Bobbie, who normally plays a grand piano, was now presented with my antique electric Wurlitzer and a cool cello-string sound; both keyboards were coming through a sweet little butterscotch Fender Deluxe guitar amplifier. I did not want to confuse Bobbie with too much technology, and I felt that giving her the job of supplying the string arrangements for the session was not only a way of complimenting her on her musical knowledge, but, selfishly speaking, was also my way of insuring that the string arrangements would be connected emotionally and played with love for Willie.

Mickey Raphael, Willie's harmonica player, also joined us. In the bottom of Mickey's harmonica box, I noticed a very large bass harmonica that I had seen before. This curious, seldom-used piece jogged my memory of early childhood. Diamond Jim's, a nightclub that I used to walk past on my way to my music lesson, displayed a marquee advertising the entertainers of the week: one week the Three Reeds, a postvaudeville novelty touring act featuring three harmonicas (including the bass harmonica), were touring through Hamilton. On the way back from my lesson, I stuck my head into Diamond Jim's and heard the magic sound of the Three Reeds. The bass harmonica, with its comical limitations—only ever one note at a time, a bit like a tuba—had a built-in feeling of fun. The Three Reeds and other traveling acts of that nature were soon to disappear. *The Ed Sullivan Show*, the most famous American variety show of the sixties, could be viewed as the last standing giant that promoted this sort of naïve variety. The Three Reeds, the Ventriloquist, the Dog Act, the Beatles and Zsa Zsa Gabor, all featured at one stop.

But variety, the spice of life in the sixties, soon splintered into compartments. At a certain point programmers decided to segregate in order to optimize their attractiveness to advertisers, aiming specific programming at specific demographics. Variety became a thing of the past. Civil rights had won many battles, but segregation within programming was on the rise.

So the harmonica was fished out of the bottom of Mickey's box and became the bass instrument on a good few songs for Willie's *Teatro*. A strange blend of active Latin drumming and singular bass harmonica notes became part of our sound, and I invited two other secret weapons: Aaron Embry and Brian

Griffiths. Aaron is a sonic inventor whom I've worked with for years, and who never fails to surprise me with the strange and wonderful. I still don't know how he does it. His toolbox is made up of found objects—thumb pianos, rare knickknacks, and antiquated cheap Casio keyboards, a nonstop jack-in-the-box of invention. And Brian is my favorite Canadian guitar player, master of the slide. I didn't invite a bass player, because I wanted to play the bass myself. Brad Mehldau (one of the great pianists of our time) also agreed to make a cameo appearance.

I made it clear to Howard that I didn't want to use any of Willie's energy for sound testing. As soon as Willie hit the chair and picked up his guitar, I wanted to be recording. Years of experience meant that telepathy was at play between Howard and me. And just like I'd pictured it, when Willie, Emmy, and I rolled in, the Teatro was ready to strike up the band.

Willie Nelson is not an artist who likes to spend a lot of time in the studio. His maverick ways are part of his music, and it would be wrong to force him to be static. To make a fast record with a lot of soul is a challenge—preparation is everything—and so the hotline between Howard and me was constantly buzzing from Willie's bus to the Teatro. Willie had written some new material, including a touching song inspired by carrying a picture of his son everywhere he went. The little photograph in a locket could be pulled out at any moment as a reminder of fatherly love toward a son. When we arrived at the Teatro, Willie stayed on the bus; in fact, Willie pretty much lives on his bus. I've seen him pull up to a hotel and never even enter it. I've heard it said that when he goes back to his ranch in Texas, he still sleeps on the bus. There is a similarity here between Willie Nelson and Bob Dylan, both tireless troubadours, both relying on the call of the road. The nonstop rolling of the wheels of Willie's bus, the nonstop turning of Bob Dylan's mind were snug harbors that had saved them time and time again from the storms of life, the moss that they had chosen to avoid. I am proud to be associated with these national treasures.

Fast records have never been my thing. I had four days to make a record with Willie Nelson. I've come up through the ranks of studio composition and invention. Willie, on the other hand, is cut from a different cloth, he carries his songs in his heart and his phrasing in his head; he is a fast operator. In order to tap into the fast-and-furious ways of Willie Nelson, I had to outsmart even myself. And so my Teatro became a time machine of sorts—a squinting of the eye had all the ghosts I needed, cheering me on in the arena. The Spanish-Cuban theme had been expressed clearly to my crew—Cuban cigars in stock, drummers preprogrammed for Latin grooves. The stage for Willie, Emmy, and me nicely set up to provide Willie with a sense of the performance hall. No headphones needed, nice full surround-sound PA, musicians and technicians on the same plane of congregation.

We opened with a guitar-and-piano Django Reinhardt–inspired feature. Willie's fingers danced across Trigger, his old faithful, well-worn Spanish guitar. The instrumental segued straight into "I'll Take You Everywhere I Go." The lovely blend of Spanish guitar and Willie's dedication of love toward his son established the direction and mood of the record; we could never lose our way. With Emmylou flawlessly following the details of Willie's unpredictable phrasing, we quickly got a take.

I can remember a Christmas at my mother's house. We had only one record to play; it was a Willie Nelson record. I was a kid then, and the vocals were strange and beautiful to my Canadian ear, but what was even stranger was Willie's phrasing. He always knows where the beat is, but the positioning of his singing flirts with the beat, sometimes behind, sometimes ahead, moving like trembling leaves in the wind. Ray Charles has the same effect on me. These masters of phrasing had not just stumbled onto their skill; years of live performance and audience response had educated them to reach this ultimate place. Dylan is the same.

Just as I suspected, my "Cuban" drummers had lit a new fire under Willie Nelson. While he waited on his bus, I would warm up the band and walk them through the grooves and arrangements of the songs. When I felt they were ready, I would go out and fetch Willie from the parking lot, and after a few general instructions we lashed into a rendition. The vocals were spotless, and the band wasn't far behind. Usually three takes max, perhaps an edit or two, provided us with a result. Quick bass overdub and then a mix as we listened back. I never take a blend for granted—blends that have a sense of purpose. An instant playback of an inspired performance usually has something to it that is relevant. A blend on a later day might be a re-creation of a vibe, but a blend on the original day draws its relevance from the physical presence of the musicians. These blends are not thought out; they are instinctive and often the most musical. All of the mixes on *Teatro* were done that way: a fast documentation of a blend relevant to the workroom.

I had to reassure the fire department that there was no fire at the Teatro; it was only a visit to Willie Nelson's bus by Woody Harrelson. I think we could safely say that the Oxnard Police Department was very accommodating in turning a blind eye to the smoke signals rising up from the Teatro. Emmylou sang like a bird, and she deserves a Grammy for her ability to follow Willie's mysterious and fascinating phrasing.

When you have quite a few musicians in a large room, you get a natural depth of field. *Teatro* is one of my favorite productions; it has a sense of presence and urgency at every turn. Brad Mehldau did make his appearance and broke everyone's heart with his piano accompaniment on a sad and wonderful song called "Home Motel." Largely driven by instinct, we blasted through twenty songs. The outtakes of *Teatro* are enough to springboard another Willie Nelson record.

Early on I could tell that our mélange held the promise of a classic, and I began to think that it might be a missed opportunity to not document such an event. A phone call to Melanie Ciccone (the force behind my business at the time) sparked the idea of inviting the great German filmmaker Wim Wenders to make a Willie Nelson film. To my surprise, Wenders said yes. He was living in Los Angeles at the time, and a fortunate window in his schedule made a filming of the Willie project possible. This was a great honor, as Wim Wenders is one of my favorite filmmakers. *Wings of Desire*; *Paris, Texas*; and *Buena Vista Social Club* are all classics that are part of me.

The Teatro had no natural light, and so it was a challenge for Wim to pull the lighting and filming crew together in time for the actual recording. We finished *Teatro*, and Willie got back on his bus. I had met the four-day deadline, and was looking forward to Willie Nelson's return for the Wim Wenders part of the project. The innocent invitation to film escalated into full-scale scaffolding, industrial lighting, Genie hoist operators, and Steadicam experts, and my cottage industry Teatro had now become a full-production Hollywood set. Our job now was to replicate the creation of the album. I now saw Wim Wenders's film as a film about a Willie Nelson performance, rather than the documentation of the making of *Teatro*.

We invited an audience and great dancers called the Pussy Cat Dolls from L.A. The idea was to now turn the Teatro into a Cuban nightclub. Willie's dance-hall instincts kicked into play. The material was fresh in our heads, and we provided Wim with the best renditions we could. Everything happened fast, everyone pretty much acting on instinct. Wim's film was not a blockbuster, but it has heart and soul. It was nominated for a Grammy.

Every now and again I bump into Willie, usually on his bus in some unexpected faraway city. His lust for life and sense of gratitude remain an inspiration to me.

18

SOUL MINING

Rooms and buildings are almost as much of an addiction for me as the music I make in them. If I didn't love architecture so much, perhaps I would be more bohemian, a wandering musician. After working on *Yellow Moon*, *Oh Mercy*, and *Acadie*, I could have left New Orleans but the architecture of the city pulled me back in. I found myself near the Mississippi River in one of the large edifices of the French Quarter at Esplanade and Chartres, one block from the French Market. My new digs, 13,000 square feet of amazing rooms and corridors and staircases. I set about turning the impressive three-story mansion into one of the great recording studios of America.

My studio had an API recording console, which I purchased from the legendary Record Plant in New York City (it was one of the largest APIs, built and customized for that studio). I purchased it in late 1989 or early 1990. Howard drove it down from New York City to New Orleans, and somehow contracted a case of the measles along the way and almost died. But he fought his way through it and made it to my place with the console intact. The closing of the Record Plant was the beginning of the landslide of a fading recording era. Their console had limited effects sends, but really good graphic equalizers (*equalizer* being a fancy name for tone control).

The API console was a discrete circuitry giant; its technology preceded the integrated circuit or silicon chip. The miracle of the silicon chip would be that you no longer needed a large circuit board of components. All those expensive components had now been reduced to a tiny, affordable chip. The electronics industry was very excited with this breakthrough, but there would be side effects—less headroom, for example, meaning less ability to handle transients or surprise loud sounds. The isolated circuitry would turn a transient or an overload into a musical effect—the sound would compress a bit and then bounce back, and it all added up to something unexpected and exciting. The new, more economical silicon chip has what you might call a threshold. If you disobey this threshold, like crossing a line drawn in the sand, you get a nasty, unmusical distortion. The silicon chip is a more affordable technology with less forgiving guidelines.

The evolution of technology always insinuates improvement. But as we saw the disappearance of this kind of console, I believe we left behind some of the best tools that record making ever had. As the giants fell, as we "progressed" from the analog to the digital, the downloads began to happen. At this point most of them are illegal, but most of the people who download would not consider themselves dishonest. I had coffee with a friend recently who said that a neighbor had come over for dinner. The neighbor brought his laptop and dumped an entire file of albums into my friend's iPod. These were not bad people. They saw themselves as file sharers. In fact, it was more music than he could listen to in a lifetime. He had entire catalogs of jazz, classics, and contemporaries. At best, my friend would skate over the surface of the many choices and likely never become intimate with someone's dedicated work. Perhaps this way of listening to music is a natural reaction to the sheer volume of fifty years of rock 'n' roll finally falling upon us.

My new New Orleans studio, the house of the API console, was meticulously managed by Karen Brady, and welcomed many incredible acts: Iggy Pop, R.E.M., Pearl Jam, and Blind Melon, to name a few of the hundreds. The great house was a crossroads for many, including a few stray dogs looking to ground themselves and write songs, like my friend Chris Whitley. I still welcome stray dogs into my house.

I had met Chris in New York City through a friend of mine, Karen Kuehn, a great New York photographer. Chris had found his voice, but not his career. I could tell he was looking for something, and I was not sure he would find it in New York. I invited him to come and live in my house in New Orleans, where I introduced him to my team and a few business folks who offered him a publishing deal that led to a record deal. With the help of Malcolm Burn, Chris made *Living with the Law*, a great first record. You can hear his haunting voice if you watch the film *Thelma and Louise*; that's him singing "Kicking Stones" as Brad Pitt is rolling in the hay with Geena Davis.

Tortured and caught in limbo between tradition and trend, Chris made his music at a time when the cowboy boot was frowned upon. His images of the big skies of Texas and his romantic association with the Dobro were not in step with the journalist's desire for the urban and the new. New York was cruel to Chris, and I was happy that he had found a place in the world, in my humble abode in New Orleans. He was a great singer and a deep soul diverted by the bottle at unfortunate moments in his career. I loved Chris, and introduced him to every opportunity that I could, including sitting at the family Christmas table in

Canada, at a time when I felt he needed a shoulder to lean on. My sister, Jocelyne, was a good friend to Chris, and we were all supporters. In the end, his body wore out and he died. I miss him and I wrote a piece of music for him called "For Chris," which I released on *Santiago*, the third volume of my Omni series.

The Omni series is a division I set up with my friend Adam Samuels, within a website called RedFloorRecords.com. Adam and I are both excited with the new technologies that enable very quick artist-to-listener contact—any artist can now have their own store. Should I decide to make available a piece of music I've just created, a simple spontaneous announcement is made on the site, and the listener can then digitally download the song. This hardly replaces the romance of record store rummaging, but there is a certain sweetness and satisfaction in bypassing the complexities of physical releases.

My friend has a seven-year-old boy. I call him Leonardo, as in "Da Vinci." Leonardo is fantastically inventive. He makes up his own little songs, loves to bounce and dance around, and writes his own stories; much the same way that I did at his age. The next chapter in his life, say nine, ten, or eleven years old, introduces new demands and expectations. If you want to be a Boy Scout, be in the school play, hang around with a certain group of friends, or play sports, you have to "fit in." One's behavior must now be modified to fit the rules of these new interests. Speaking for myself, when I decided to become a navy cadet, I had to wear the uniform and march in the way that they taught me to fit into their club. It's part of human nature to want to fit in, but the more that we fit in, the less individualistic we become.

It will be a sad day for me if Leonardo ever loses his imaginative inclinations in order to "fit in" . . . but we all do, the irony of it being that we want to seem fabulously unique and original by the time we get to be twenty.

A few years back, my hometown university very kindly presented me with an honorary Ph.D. Once I got past the tasseled chapeau and the photo with Mom, I was left with the dean's compliment. He said to me that he hopes his university students reach my place of accomplishment. I assumed that he meant a place of passion and individuality, the very components strongly driving Leonardo.

Present day: workaholic tendencies still intact. But maybe being a workaholic is a good thing. After all this, getting in a van full of equipment—driving to Las Vegas to get in the trenches one more time—would seem like a good idea. Yes, at the peak of my career, pulling into a strip mall. Old carpets and coffee stains, empty pizza boxes and lots of Slurpees . . . Yes, in the studio one more time. This time with Brandon Flowers from the Killers.

Razor-sharp kind of guy, musicologist by labor and self-appointment, the stories unfold as I get to know my new friend. I see the honesty and beauty in him and immediately understand that he is driven by the right engine. If his good values can enter the music, then we should be all right. Nobody thinks of Las Vegas as a place where talent comes from. Normally Las Vegas has talent visiting. I can hear Brandon's influences, and that's okay by me; we all got into this because we fell in love with already existing works. The part of me that looks for the original turns a blind eye to the influences and a good eye to the imagination of this young man. Aha, he's a storyteller! There it is, the never-ending frontier—storytelling. Life experience lives beyond the medium.

We have a good couple of fast days, as the rise of Brandon Flowers and his way of looking at the world becomes my point of interest. He talks about dreaming as a young boy; he tells me about leaving home at sixteen to come to the big city of Las Vegas. His new home, his aunt's house, had a piano in it. Brandon had just found the key to his creative future. His story reminds me of my own. I encourage him to write a song about his calling. Images of black hills, desertscape, hard work, teenage love, early-days Vegas, Brandon busing tables, echoes of my pin-setting days bump up against Brandon's, a song starts unfolding. We huddle up in the band room; a performance erupts, a journey starts, five minutes later the story is told. We laugh about the pitfalls of the spontaneous arrangement, but there is magic there. Magic in the front and magic in the back. Cut out a bit of the middle and nobody notices the fat. Back at the hotel, physical exhaustion, margaritas, and gamblers, to bed and then more coffee.

The phone rings; Neil Young is on the line. Would I record an acoustic record for him? Yes, I would. I've been waiting all my life to make a Neil Young record. Full moon is on the rise, Neil Young is in the drive. My team and I are ready to surprise Neil with new sounds. Neil gets hooked on the mechanics of my experiments. He hears sounds he's never heard before. The acoustic record has just gone electro. Same old beast, tandem tradition and future. Neil sings about love and war, about a polar bear floating on an iceberg, about the coming of industry to America, about the rivers drinking the poison of our waste. He sings about love of man, about the dancing waves of the ocean. He loves the guitar as I do. We rummage through my collection of handpicked guitar amplifiers and accessories—two kids in a candy store. Down-on-all-fours-interfacing, Sears-catalog-order gadgets mixed with high-end professional equipment. My Canadian temperament seems to suit my Canadian friend. The full moon passes eight songs later. Neil and I agree to hook back up on the next moon.

I always felt that the rhythmic part of me had not been fully tapped into, and so when a phone call came from a young R & B artist by the name of Ne-Yo, I felt that my chance had finally come. West Hollywood, coffee stains and pizza boxes, suspicion and then hand-slapping, rifling through a lobby of posse. The secret door in the cork-lined wall reveals the man himself. Ne-Yo, cut, sharply dressed, explains to me that he doesn't like what's on radio; he wants to make a difference. Howard pulls into the back alley with a purple van full of my gear. Pretty Tony is there too. We set up and start. Ne-Yo spots something in my guitar playing that he likes; my riff suggests a groove. He bangs the bass drum part with his hand on the console—Pretty Tony mimics. I steal a diminished chord from Neil Young, and maybe Brandon Flowers is in there, too. Maybe we are like Keith Haring or Banksy, picking up influences that sooner or later come bursting back out. Ne-Yo hums a melody, I work it into the guitar part. We decide on an arrangement and lash into a first take . . . and then it happens, like I've never seen before. In half an hour, Ne-Yo has a finished lyric. The second take is fully fleshed out—Ne-Yo's phrasing is the best. I wonder what goes on in this young man's mind.

This is where it gets interesting. To excel at something is to have seen an open door to an idea. With all my experience, I have never gone where Ne-Yo has gotten to. At another time he might have been a little Mozart or a little Beethoven. His understanding of harmony is greater than mine. Ne-Yo needs no encouragement, like Neil Young doesn't want encouragement. They know what needs to be done, like a fighter going in for another round. Encouragement from your corner will not provide the blow necessary to be champion. As the sweat rolls off, you see that momentary chance to get in and strike. Ne-Yo layers his harmony parts with full knowledge of what has been and what will be. The chorus is a good chorus, but becomes a great chorus by the time Ne-Yo is done. My little church in a suitcase is ready for garnishing. A bit of processing and I have it sounding like a Trinidadian steel drum. Ne-Yo lights up; he has never heard this sound before. The climate is urban, but the soul is old. The soul in our piece of music has church in it. A bit of church in West Hollywood is not so bad. The day is done; we pile into the purple van and head back to Silverlake.

Neil Young is on the phone. He wants to know if I can locate him some guitar strings that he can't find anymore. Strings and tubes and amps, chasing grounds, buzzes, and hums. It may be a fast and technological world, but we still work with finger articulation and the never-ending frontier—the lyrical journey. Ne-Yo, Neil, Brandon, and I all come from very different places, but in the end we are happy to get our hands dirty.

A roaring amount of decibels rings in the lobby of Bella Vista. I think I hear Neil Young's '58 El Dorado pulsing up the herringbone drive. Let's get ready, because it's gonna be good under full moon and forever skies.

I thank God for giving me the ability to be excited. Sometimes I think it's the only fuel I have to run on. If I'm in the right mood, inspiration comes to me in the strangest ways. Music is, of course, the main thing that I do and what people know me for, but music never starts with just music. It starts with inspiration. Looking in the face of someone doing janitorial work can bring me inspiration: maybe the janitor has found happiness in the humdrum, because he gets to go home and feed his kids, maybe the janitor knows how to whistle better than me. He knows the song of gratitude. Half a life of suffering in another country has made him very grateful to have any income at all. The janitor sees the sky, and breathes the miracle air, and is happy to be alive. He may not be a songwriter, but I am. I feel that it's my responsibility to write a song of gratitude for this janitor and others like him who may not be fortunate enough to ever hold an instrument in their hands. A bird on a wire is a symbol of freedom, if you take the time to look up.

Some of us were not born to belong to this time. The contemporary urban demands placed upon us may not consider the fragile heart. In a village, the fragile heart might have a better chance of survival, because he has a built-in watchful eye from friends and relatives. Some of the homeless people that I've gotten to know in Los Angeles, for example, have brilliant minds that simply could not respond to the fundamental "red tape" demands of big cities. A hardworking wheat-field worker should be loved and accepted for the value of his work. That same person in downtown Los Angeles might be sleeping under a cardboard box in the cold.

In 2003 I gave the keynote address at the South by Southwest music festival in Austin, Texas. My speech, called "Soul Mining," was fueled with fantasia and images of climbing down a mine shaft looking for gold and gems in the midst of debris; it was meant to be an analogy for anyone trudging through the mire, looking for dignity and quality (in anything, really). Quality is a lifelong quest, and I've run along with enough dedicated hopefuls to be regarded as part of the team that has gone thirsty looking for that artesian well at the end of a long desert.

My little brother had died two days before, and I almost canceled my keynote speech, but in the end, in the name of little Ronnie, I persisted, and in my own quiet way, I dedicated the speech to him, as he was a soul searching for dignity and for a place in the world where he could be a significant contributor to life and quality. Chris Whitley himself died not long after. Now that this somber part is out of the way, I can carry on talking about hopes and dreams for the living. And so my dedication to my brother:

SOUL MINING

Why has Danny Lanois been invited to speak here in Austin at the convention?

They must think he knows something.

The French Canadian kid who put a recording studio in the basement of his mother's house, with his brother Bob, and proceeded to make hundreds of albums—he must know something. About feel, time, crackles and buzzes, magnetic field.

He must know how to tune a piano, how to tune a drum kit.

He must know that the 24-inch Zildjian is different from the Paiste.

He must know that sometimes you have to go next door and pay off the neighbor to get him to stop cutting the grass so you can finish your vocal overdub.

He must know that you gotta say something when it all seems wrong.

He must know that when someone tells you you can't do something, you prove them wrong—that you smile and you find out how to get in the back door.

He must know that you help people, give guidance, and without any expectation you give it your all, and then one day someone calls you a record producer, and invitations come.

It's like baking—you mix invitation with preparation, and like magic you get a big fat cherry pie. Somebody eats the cherry pie and they ask for more and you can honestly look them in the eye and say, there's plenty more where that came from.

Danny Lanois knows that the cherry pie was there to celebrate years of soul mining, going down deep, looking for that moment that might make a difference, eyes practically shut from coal dust, looking for that original fragment that will give a piece of music a chance to be recognized as unique.

That feeling you get when you are walking on the street and you hear a song and you can say, Yeah, that's the one—that one that's different from all the others. The people who made that record found something fresh and unique, some way of looking at the world and letting everybody else in on it.

And then Danny Lanois goes down a little deeper, more dust in the eyes, looking for another glimmer. He goes down and hears the sound of a drum beating the senses across the back with a stick. Somebody is pounding the vacant industrial neighborhood of Dublin, oblivious to the easy, breezy contamination of radio, their hearts resonating with the belief that they can make a difference with caring.

Little Danny Lanois is there hanging on to old values—wearing the hands of a bricklayer, getting up early, chasing away crackles and hums, wondering why the computer fan is so damn noisy in the control room where we will be singing on the day, wondering why the stupidity of the in-line console has managed to become the standard of the industry.

He challenges the elitism of the control room.

Why not make the ergonomics of the recording studio such

that they be public to the members of the band? Are we not here to have a common language, to facilitate ease of operation? I want the guitar player to be the engineer if he wants, for the arrangement of the song to be open for discussion—no hidden information, no shared functions. I don't want my steering wheel to be my brake pedal.

Then Danny Lanois goes digging deeper in the soul mine and there it is—the mother lode. Sitting in the corner of the room, wearing glasses, that seemingly silent voice that suddenly becomes the musical identity of the song, that sonic signature that will allow all of us to recognize that song from across the street. He harnesses it, stops the press, puts the kid wearing the glasses up on the pedestal and says, You are great and this is your song—this is your moment of originality. I'm going to do everything in my power to let the world hear it, but it is only the beginning—the idea is rough and is going to need labor, love, and building.

We shake off the coal dust and imagine that there are other people in the world who want to feel the way we feel right now. We have synchronicity in our favor—we believe we see the future. And at a time when everything seems to sound the same—a voice of a generation is born, the channeling is open wide, the future is bright and clear, the baby-face killer mixing with the burning spear.

Chris Blackwell with little Bob Marley—coming in to display their wares of soul mining. New Orleans radio reached the shores of Jamaica and osmosis once again shook the genes of invention—in the absence of regulation, in the hands of disc jockeys, our spirits were lifted.

Farther down the mine shaft I bump into Jimmy Iovine. I say, Jimmy, you're looking good. He says, I'll tell you why I'm looking good—I eat dinner with my kids, we don't spend our lives in restaurants around here—we spend our lives making records.

Johnny Cash walked in and said, What's all the fuss—can't you keep it close to the bone—and he lashed into the Tennessee stud.

I promised myself to be reincarnated as the man in black
where crickets are chirping—the water is high
there's a soft cotton dress—on the line hangin' dry
windows wide open—African trees
bent over backward—from a hurricane breeze
not a word of goodbye—not even a note
she's gone with the man in the long black coat
farther down the shaft Leonard Cohen is working with Dre
some kind of thing just another way to say
the word is still the final frontier
the word belongs to anybody
don't need cash to tell your story—don't need cash to worry
don't need cash to know the feeling
of four kids being raised on a hairdresser's salary—me one of them—
so I went farther down the shaft without the comfort of college
without the reassurance of any business community
just the will and the presence of my brother Bob
we brainstormed and said—what if—what if—what if
until we were there looking at Brian Eno—who said, Master your simple tools and make your music
low baggage—high mileage—passion before commerce—intelligence before waste
the four-track, acting as a door stop, talks back
Geoff Emerick doesn't know how he did it
he used 8 tracks, we need 108
Emmylou Harris and Porter Wagoner walk in and ask

me—Why did *Soul Train* sound better than the David Letterman show?
I tell them that the race to the extension of the high-frequency part of the spectrum is choking the shadows of the bass
if you light your picture too bright you will lose your shadows
Danny Lanois went deeper down the shaft to where there was silence and his ears were pure
so pure there was no music—you couldn't hear anything
it was a luxury of deafness—a kind of cotton wool
and in that lower level—that cave—he saw ten strings and a piece of green maple
he picked it up and he prayed that something would lift him up out of the claws of debris—
the plastic faces pretending to be speaking melted
hidden-agenda lifestyle protection hypocrisy faded
people spoke the truth and told it like it is
the voice of Aaron Neville made a mockery of injustice
little Jimi Hendrix—James Brown and Willie Nelson
had a hit called humanitarian efforts
and so I pick up the piece of green maple with ten strings
and I practice and put my heart and soul into every note
my passion becomes the same as the one I felt at nine years old
I invite everyone here this morning to ignite—reignite—or just plain old turn up the flame in what you believe in and get to the top of the mountain that you see
invention is in your brain—
and that never-ending commodity is in the bottom of your heart—

it's called passion.
Danny Lanois is going down one more time with coal dust
    in his eyes
going down—
soul mining.

ACKNOWLEDGMENTS

I was reluctant to write a book because I'm not a book writer, but I am a songwriter, and songs tell stories. On the strength of the storytelling part of things, I decided to give the book a try. After a couple of test chapters, I found that there was something in there that could at least be inspiring to somebody else. Simply put, the driving force behind the work seemed as interesting as the work itself.

Thank you to all my friends who are included in this book who didn't get a chance to tell their side of the story. Members of the cast: Eno, U2, Billy Bob Thornton, Harry Dean Stanton, Wim Wenders, Bob Dylan, Emmylou Harris, Willie Nelson, Leonard Cohen, Peter Gabriel, Jimmy Cliff, Rick James, Raffi, Chris Blackwell, Robbie Robertson, the Neville Brothers, Ne-Yo, Brandon Flowers, Neil Young, my family, my mother, Gilberte, my brother Bob, my brother Ron, my sister, Jocelyne, Brian Patti, Jennifer Tefft, James May, Brian Blade, Mark Howard, Pretty Tony Mangurian, Jim Keltner, Aaron Embry, Malcolm Burn, Adam Samuels, and Chris Whitley.

I'd like to thank my anti-sabotage team: Margaret Marissen,

who takes care of my business in Toronto; Keisha Kalfin, who helped me write the book; and the girls at Faber and Faber, Denise Oswald, Chantal Clarke, and Mitzi Angel. Thanks to Ava Stander for making the introduction to Faber, to Bettina Rosenthal for her longtime friendship and encouragement to write the book, and to Tomaz Jardim, Renee Pietrangelo, and Cathy Cutz for their support. I'd also like to thank all my photographer friends for their kindness: Donata Wenders, Danny Clinch, Christina Alicino, Colm Henry, Jennifer Tipoulow, Bob Lanois, Gilberte Lanois, Adam Vollick, Keisha Kalfin, and any photographers whom we may have overlooked.

INDEX